Implementing Grand Strategy in Asia Through Institutions

An Exploratory Analysis

RAFIQ DOSSANI, LYNN HU, CHRISTIAN CURRIDEN

Sponsored by the Korea Foundation

NATIONAL SECURITY RESEARCH DIVISION

For more information on this publication, visit **www.rand.org/t/RRA1653-1**.

About RAND

The RAND Corporation is a research organization that develops solutions to public policy challenges to help make communities throughout the world safer and more secure, healthier and more prosperous. RAND is nonprofit, nonpartisan, and committed to the public interest. To learn more about RAND, visit www.rand.org.

Research Integrity

Our mission to help improve policy and decisionmaking through research and analysis is enabled through our core values of quality and objectivity and our unwavering commitment to the highest level of integrity and ethical behavior. To help ensure our research and analysis are rigorous, objective, and nonpartisan, we subject our research publications to a robust and exacting quality-assurance process; avoid both the appearance and reality of financial and other conflicts of interest through staff training, project screening, and a policy of mandatory disclosure; and pursue transparency in our research engagements through our commitment to the open publication of our research findings and recommendations, disclosure of the source of funding of published research, and policies to ensure intellectual independence. For more information, visit www.rand.org/about/principles.

RAND's publications do not necessarily reflect the opinions of its research clients and sponsors.

About This Report

This report studies how China implements its grand strategy in Asia using institutions. To address this question, we first reviewed the literature on China's grand strategy, its use of institutions, and its emphasis on Asia. We then turned to policy experts to discuss China's use of institutions to implement its grand strategy toward Asian nations of interest to China, including, as a case study, the countries of the Korean Peninsula.

Our findings are as follows: China's grand strategy since the end of the Cold War has consistently been guided by its long-term goal of building a pre-eminent Asian presence and a larger global presence in the socioeconomic, diplomatic, and defense arenas. To achieve this goal, China currently desires to accomplish three outcomes: (1) achieve greater economic integration with Asia and the rest of the world, (2) manage its rivalry with the United States, and (3) build soft power globally.

The desired outcomes have changed over the past three decades in response to changing circumstances within and outside China. China's strategies to achieve its desired outcomes have also evolved in turn. One main strategic change is China's increased use of multilateral, regional, and bilateral institutions to address the socioeconomic, diplomatic, and national security dimensions of China's interests. China has found regional and bilateral institutions particularly important for its implementation of strategy in Asia.

In our case study, we find that China mostly uses institutions to accomplish greater economic integration with both North and South Korea. To manage its rivalry with the United States in the Korean Peninsula, as well as build soft power, China uses both institutional and noninstitutional initiatives. We draw from these findings to derive several implications—both for the adequacy of China's institutions-based approach and for the responses by middle powers.

RAND National Security Research Division

This research was sponsored by the Korea Foundation under its Policy Oriented Research Program and conducted within the International Security and Defense Policy Center of the RAND National Security Research Division (NSRD), which operates the National Defense Research Institute (NDRI), a federally funded research and development center sponsored by the Office of the Secretary of Defense, the Joint Staff, the Unified Combatant Commands, the Navy, the Marine Corps, the defense agencies, and the defense intelligence enterprise.

For more information on the RAND International Security and Defense Policy Center, see www.rand.org/nsrd/isdp or contact the director (contact information is provided on the webpage).

Acknowledgments

The authors acknowledge the support of the Korea Foundation. We would like to thank the interviewees, all of whom gave generously of their time and knowledge to convey their understanding of this difficult topic. Finally, we thank the reviewers of this report, Cortez Cooper, Andrew Scobell, and David Shambaugh, for their time, expertise, and diligence.

Summary

China's economic growth has been accompanied by a rise in its regional and global ambitions. It has sought to fulfill these ambitions in various ways, including through the promotion of new initiatives and institutions. For example, the trillion-dollar Belt and Road Initiative (BRI), with its constitutional mandate and support from leading Chinese institutions, has propelled China into the central role of providing development finance—a role traditionally played by the United States and other developed countries—by creating a set of Chinese-funded land and sea infrastructure corridors that link China to Asia and Europe.

Some of these initiatives may accomplish multiple outcomes. For example, in addition to providing development finance to developing countries, the BRI's corridors integrate China's economy more closely with those of developing countries. Through the land corridors, China could transport its goods to Asia and Europe if maritime routes, which are currently the main routes for transport, are blockaded in a war.

The large number of new institutions and initiatives that China, in recent years, has chosen to promote or be actively involved in suggests that its grand strategy may have changed. What is this grand strategy, how does it involve institutions, and what are its implications for Asia?

To address these questions, we first reviewed the literature on China's grand strategy, its use of institutions, and its emphasis on Asia. We then turned to policy experts to discuss China's use of institutions in implementing its grand strategy toward Asian nations of interest to China, including, as a case study, the countries of the Korean Peninsula.

We find that China's grand strategy since the end of the Cold War has consistently been guided by one long-term goal. That long-term goal is to build a pre-eminent Asian presence and a growing global presence in the socioeconomic, diplomatic, and defense arenas. To achieve this goal, China currently desires to accomplish three outcomes: (1) achieve greater economic integration with Asia and the rest of the world, (2) manage its rivalry with the United States, and (3) build soft power globally.

The desired outcomes have changed over the past three decades in response to changing circumstances within and outside China and are now more interdependent than they ever were. First, China's strategic focus now covers all of Asia, whereas earlier, its strategic emphasis was on Southeast and Northeast Asia. This change is driven by economic needs, such as access to mineral resources, and security needs, such as securing its borders with Central Asian states.

A second change is that economic integration has replaced trade openness both for Asia and globally. This change is being accomplished primarily through outbound foreign direct investment (FDI), in which China now ranks as a world leader.

Third, because relations with the United States have changed to become more competitive, China needs to manage this rivalry rather than, as before, cultivate the United States as a partner for trade and strategic dialogue. The decades-old "America factor" in China's grand strategy continues to loom large, but its dimensions have spread into new areas, such as maritime competition in Asian seas and offsetting U.S. influence in Asia through FDI.

Fourth, China seeks soft power engagement globally, whereas earlier, China targeted this ambition at the developing world.

China's strategies to achieve its desired outcomes have evolved in tandem. One of the main changes is China's increased use of institutions. From a survival-driven, largely noninstitutional approach during the Cold War, China has come to use institutions more extensively (though not exclusively) thereafter to address the socioeconomic, diplomatic, and national security dimensions of China's interests. These institutions are multilateral, regional, and bilateral in nature and include both institutions that existed prior to China's involvement with them and new institutions. The latter group includes institutions that China has initiated or co-promoted—sometimes in competition with existing institutions. China has found regional and bilateral institutions to be particularly important for the implementation of its grand strategy in Asia.

In our case study, we find that China mostly uses institution-based strategies to accomplish greater economic integration with both North and South Korea. To manage its rivalry with the United States in the Korean Peninsula as well as build soft power, China uses both institutional and noninstitutional initiatives.

China's institutions-based grand strategy raises important issues for middle Asian powers like South Korea. These issues require such countries to choose between working with Chinese economic institutions or diversifying their economies to be less dependent on China and between accepting Chinese primacy in addressing their security needs or building their own coalitions.

Contents

Figure and Tables

Figure

Tables

CHAPTER ONE

Introduction

China's rapid economic growth in recent years has been based on an increasing level of economic integration[1] with other countries, particularly the countries of Southeast and Northeast Asia. As China has grown economically, its regional and global ambitions have gone beyond economic integration to encompass the attainment of technological, diplomatic, cultural, and military power.

From the manifestations of these ambitions through socioeconomic, soft power, diplomatic, and military initiatives, may we glean a distinct *grand strategy* that aims to enable China's attainment of great power status? The large number of new institutions and initiatives that China, in recent years, has chosen to promote or be actively involved in (see Table 3.1 in Chapter Three) suggests that its grand strategy has evolved, and this exploratory study examines how.

We find that China's grand strategy since the end of the Cold War has been guided by one long-term goal. That long-term goal is to build a pre-eminent Asian presence and a growing global presence in the socioeconomic, diplomatic, and defense arenas. To achieve this goal, China currently desires to accomplish three outcomes: (1) achieve greater economic integration with Asia and the rest of the world, (2) manage its rivalry with the United States, and (3) build soft power globally.

The desired outcomes have changed over the past three decades in response to changing circumstances within and outside China and are now more interdependent than they ever were. First, China's focus now covers all of Asia, whereas earlier, its emphasis was on Southeast and Northeast Asia. This change is driven by economic needs, such as access to mineral resources, and security needs, such as securing China's borders with Central Asian states.

A second change is that economic integration has replaced trade openness both for Asia and globally. This change is being accomplished primarily through outbound foreign direct investment (FDI), in which China now ranks as a world leader.

Third, because relations with the United States have become more competitive in recent years, China needs to manage this rivalry. After the Cold War ended, China's security concerns centered on the power that a unipolar world gave to the United States. It cultivated the United States as a partner, with both countries agreeing to establish a strategic partnership in

---

[1] For a definition of this and other key terms, see the Glossary (Appendix B).

1997, thanks to expanding trade relations and regular strategic dialogues. This relationship started changing into a more competitive one during the Obama administration, which led China to adopt new strategies, such as maritime competition with the United States in Asia.

Fourth, China now seeks soft power engagement globally, whereas earlier, China targeted this ambition at the developing world.

China's plans to achieve its desired outcomes have, in turn, also evolved over time. One of the main changes is its increased use of institutions. From a survival-driven, largely non-institutional approach during the Cold War, China has come to use institutions more actively (though not exclusively) thereafter to address the socioeconomic, diplomatic, and national security dimensions of China's interests. These institutions are multilateral, regional, and bilateral in nature and include both institutions that existed prior to China's involvement with them and new institutions. The latter group includes institutions that China has initiated or co-promoted—sometimes in competition with existing institutions.

China has found regional and bilateral institutions to be particularly important for the implementation of its grand strategy in Asia. For example, China's Belt and Road Initiative (BRI), a trillion-dollar constitutionally mandated, institutionally supported initiative that was launched in 2013, seeks to connect China to other parts of Asia and the rest of the world through rail, power, and other infrastructure linkages (Ministry of Foreign Affairs of the People's Republic of China, 2013; Xinhua News Agency, 2017). The BRI has already demonstrated the potential to help poor countries accelerate their development and has put China firmly at the center of world development finance. In 2020, the United States committed $1.5 billion to finance overseas infrastructure projects (U.S. International Development Finance Corporation, undated). By comparison, China's overseas infrastructure spending through the BRI alone is about $40 billion per year and its commitments exceed $1 trillion (Organisation for Economic Co-Operation and Development [OECD], 2018).

Asia is the largest recipient of BRI funds, at 54 percent, followed by Africa at 27 percent. The leading Asian countries to receive BRI investment are Pakistan, Vietnam, and Indonesia, while the leading region for investment in Africa is Sub-Saharan Africa (Nedopil, 2021). These are all developing countries. Through the BRI, China seems to be addressing an important soft power objective, which is to be seen as the champion of the Global South.

The BRI may help accomplish two other outcomes as well. For example, the BRI's corridors could integrate China's economy more closely with those of developing countries. Through its land corridors, China could transport its goods to Asia and Europe if maritime routes, which are currently the main routes for transport, are blockaded in a war.

Another notable example of China's institution-based strategy is the Shanghai Cooperation Organisation (SCO), a regional group of governments with socioeconomic, diplomatic, counterterrorism, and military goals (SCO, undated). Initiated by China and established in 2001, the SCO has nine member countries as of 2021. It achieved significant success in addressing counterterrorism and border issues in its early years. Counterterrorism continues to be a significant activity of the SCO. Its new focus areas, as described in a 2020 declaration, include building diplomatic consensus regarding the security issues of regional and neighboring states, such as Syria, and the need for "shaping a multipolar world order"— both statements are indicative of efforts to manage the China-U.S. (and Russia-U.S.) rivalry (Al-Qahtani, 2006; Atlantic Council, undated; SCO, undated). Is the SCO a key element of China's grand strategy?

Given China's size, economic and military power, and economic interdependence with several countries in Asia—particularly those in Northeast Asia and Southeast Asia—China's grand strategy could have implications for the region. This raises the following questions: What is China's grand strategy? What are the manifestations and implications of that grand strategy for Asia? How might other Asian states respond to China's grand strategy?

Organization of This Report

Our approach to addressing the above questions is as follows. We first reviewed the literature on grand strategy (Chapter Two), with a focus on China's grand strategy, its use of institutions, and its emphasis on Asia (Chapter Three). Next, we turned to experts from the policy-making and scholarly communities to review China's use of institutions in implementing its grand strategy toward Asian nations of interest to China (Chapter Three). We then developed a case study of China's grand strategy as it affects the Korean Peninsula (Chapter Four). Our study findings are synthesized in Chapter Five.

CHAPTER TWO

Defining Grand Strategy

Along the lines of Goldstein (2020),[1] we define *grand strategy* as a national plan to coordinate and direct a nation's resources at the highest levels toward the attainment of some national goal, with specified resources and associated timelines.

Grand strategy has three primary characteristics (Silove, 2018). The first is its long-term nature. As Paul Kennedy (1991) states, grand strategy is "about the evolution and integration of policies that should operate for decades, or even for centuries (p. 4)." This suggests that grand strategy goals ought to be relatively constant over time.

A second characteristic of grand strategy is its holistic and integrated nature, which involves all the resources of a state (Hart, 1967). The more modern term for this is *whole-of-government strategy*, which includes the state's military, diplomatic, technological, and economic resources.

The third characteristic of grand strategy is that its purpose is to advance national security, i.e., as Makinda (1996) puts it, "the preservation of the state's territorial integrity and external sovereignty" (p. 152) or, as Posen (2003) puts it, to maintain a country's global "power position" (p. 8).

For small or middle powers, their grand strategy needs to be sensitive to great power interests. For example, South Korea's occasional pursuit of unification with North Korea after the Korean War (1950–1953) was affected by the actions of its more powerful 1953 treaty ally, the United States. While the Cold War was ongoing, the U.S. interest in containing the Soviet Union, with which North Korea was allied, effectively prevented South Korean initiatives toward unification. Since 1992, unification efforts restarted but have been held back, in part, by U.S. concerns about North Korean nuclear weapons (Wit, 2001).[2]

Even for great powers, autonomy is never absolute unless they have unipolar power. As Scobell et al. (2020, p. 6) notes, a great power's grand strategy is often intertwined with a

---

[1] Goldstein (2020, p. 166) defines *grand strategy* as "the combination of political-diplomatic, economic, and military means that a state embraces to ensure its vital interests and pursue its goals." He further notes that "grand strategy is distinguished in part by its broad scope as an overarching vision about a regime's top priorities and how they can be met by drawing on the various policy instruments at its disposal."

[2] The nuclear disarmament issue is, of course, just one factor in the larger reunification discussion. Political, economic, and other factors specific to the two Korean nations could play major roles, even if a nuclear disarmament agreement was reached.

state's perceived or actual rivalry with another state. For instance, during the Cold War, the Soviet Union's and the United States' grand strategies were interdependent. Each country had its own regional and global security interests, but its strategic expression depended heavily on its rival's grand strategy. Although grand strategy does not need a rival or enemy to exist, according to one view, "national strategies historically have been predicated on the existence of an enemy that needs to be overcome" (Sibii, undated).

An important manifestation of grand strategy is the use of institutions. North (1991, p. 97) defines *institutions* as "the humanly devised constraints that structure political, economic and social interaction. They consist of both informal constraints (sanctions, taboos, customs, traditions, and codes of conduct), and formal rules (constitutions, laws, property rights)."

National and multilateral institutions can help nations fulfill long-term goals. For example, U.S. provision of foreign aid, a long-term goal, is channeled via national agencies, such as the U.S. Agency for International Development, as well as via multilateral institutions, such as the aid agencies of the United Nations (UN). In response to the COVID-19 pandemic, China announced $50 million in aid to the World Health Organization, apart from around $3 billion through its own agencies, primarily the China International Development Cooperation Agency (CIDCA), established in 2018 (CIDCA, undated; Ravelo, 2017; Rudyak, 2019; Ministry of Foreign Affairs of the People's Republic of China, 2021).

Although institutions are not the only way to implement a national plan, they have some advantages over noninstitutional approaches, as follows (Zucker, 1983; North, 1991):

- **Long-term commitment to objectives and rules:** Institutions force the member states to make commitments on a rules-bound, long-term basis to the objectives of the institutions. Institutions thus allow members to project themselves as responsible, long-term players. This can also be a source of reassurance to smaller members of an institution regarding how bigger members will exercise their power.
- **Expertise:** Institutions enable the creation of a reservoir of expertise that outlives a particular leadership.
- **Standard-setting and transparency:** Institutions enable other states to join the institution, provided that they meet its standards and rules. This can help raise standards in the new member state while also allowing for the pooling of expertise and resources.
- **Management of public goods:** Regarding multilateral institutions, such institutions help member nations fulfill their collective responsibility toward global public goods, such as the environment.

Of course, institutions are not free of disadvantages relative to noninstitutional approaches. The main advantages of noninstitutional initiatives are that they (1) **accomplish short-term objectives** without tying up resources for the long term; (2) **restrict membership** to a group of pre-identified interested parties, which enables coalitions to be organized quickly; and (3) **enable experimentation** with new approaches and new partners as a precursor to institutionalization. Table 2.1 shows examples of prominent international institutions and non-

TABLE 2.1

Some Key International Institutions and Noninstitutional Initiatives

Institution Name	Type of Institution	Objective Type	Advantage
Institutional initiatives			
UN and its agencies	Multilateral	Diplomatic, socioeconomic, and security	• Long-term commitment to objectives and rules • Expertise • Standard-setting and transparency • Management of public goods
WTO	Intergovernmental and global	Economic	• Long-term commitment to objectives and rules • Expertise • Standard-setting and transparency
WB, IMF	Intergovernmental and global	Economic	• Long-term commitment to objectives and rules • Expertise • Standard-setting and transparency
ASEAN	Intergovernmental and regional	Diplomatic and socioeconomic	• Long-term commitment to objectives and rules
SCO	Intergovernmental and regional	Diplomatic, socioeconomic, and security	• Long-term commitment to objectives and rules
NATO, ANZUS, Rio Treaty	Intergovernmental and regional	Security	• Long-term commitment to objectives and rules
Security Treaty—U.S.-Japan, U.S.-Korea, U.S.-Philippines, U.S.-Thailand	Intergovernmental and bilateral	Security	• Long-term commitment to objectives and rules
Noninstitutional initiatives			
Coalition of the Willing	Intergovernmental and global (informal)	Security	• Accomplish short-term objectives • Restricted membership
Quadrilateral Security Dialogue	Intergovernmental and regional (informal)	Diplomatic, security	• Restricted membership • Precursor to institutionalization
Free and Open Indo-Pacific	Intergovernmental and regional (informal)	Diplomatic, security	• Restricted membership
G7	Intergovernmental and global (informal)	Diplomatic	• Restricted membership
BRI	Intergovernmental, bilateral, and regional	Economic and diplomatic	• Precursor to institutionalization

institutional initiatives, their objectives, and their advantages (Kastner, Pearson, and Rector, 2018; Johnston, 2014).

The difference between the institutional initiatives and the noninstitutional initiatives listed in Table 2.1 lies in the adherence to formal rules of engagement. The Association of Southeast Asian Nations (ASEAN), for instance, is governed by its charter, which defines the scope of membership, objectives, and mode of functioning. By contrast, the Group of 7 (G7), which does not have its own website, is an informal association whose members have come together based on shared values. Unlike a rules-bound entity, these values do not formally define the scope of membership or specify objectives and the mode of functioning (ASEAN, undated; G7 UK, undated).

The advantages of institutions have made them an important component of nations' strategic toolkits. In the next chapter, we look at China's grand strategy and discuss its use of institutions.

CHAPTER THREE

China's Grand Strategy—An Increased Reliance on Institutions

In this chapter, we focus on the goals, desired outcomes, and plans of China's grand strategy, and how these developed from China's and the world's changing circumstances. We find that China's goals have remained unchanged since the end of the Cold War, but achieving those goals has necessitated significant changes in China's desired outcomes and new strategies and plans.

The literature generally agrees that, at the present time, as Scobell et al. (2020) puts it, China's "central goals are to produce a China that is well governed, socially stable, economically prosperous, technologically advanced, and militarily powerful by 2050" (p. ix). Or, as Goldstein (2020) states, the "enduring purpose" of China's grand strategy from the end of the Cold War to the present time has been "rejuvenation—to regain its standing as an advanced country and a great power" (p. 169).

During the Cold War, China's goal was more modest: "Beijing's overriding challenge was to ensure a relatively weak China's security in the face of pressing threats from the superpowers" (Goldstein, 2001, p. 835). This weakness arose from the disruption of the economy during the Cultural Revolution (1966–1976). Initially, to address its security concerns, China allied with the Soviet Union (Goldstein, 2001). After the China-Soviet split in the 1960s, China sought closer relations to the United States to protect itself from the Soviet Union (Kraus, 2020), a process that was formalized with U.S. recognition of the People's Republic of China in 1972. This situation continued until the Cold War ended, by which time China's rift with the Soviet Union had also healed.

Since 1979, China has focused on national development. Under Deng Xiaoping, China undertook several reforms that opened the economy to market-driven development. Although there were some significant foreign policy challenges during this time, such as the aftermath of the Tiananmen Square crackdown of 1989, China was able to manage these issues while focusing on its economic development.

After the Cold War ended, China's security concerns centered on the power that a unipolar world gave to the United States. Goldstein (2001, p. 840) writes that

> [t]he potential threat from a hostile U.S. topped the list of Beijing's newly acute security concerns. After the demise of its Soviet rival, an unchecked U.S. . . . was free to under-

take repeated military interventions around the globe. Most worrying was its decision to dispatch two aircraft carrier battle groups to the area around Taiwan in response to China's coercive diplomacy during 1995–96 intended to weaken separatist sentiment on the island.

In a similar vein, Freeman discusses China's preoccupation with the United States as a cause of some of China's strategic responses (Freeman, 2018; Freeman, 2020).

As the shadow of the Tiananmen Square crackdown of 1989 started to fade in the face of China's continued economic growth, China started attracting U.S. attention in a positive way. President Clinton called for increased economic engagement with China in 1994 (Goldstein, 2001). China welcomed the opportunity for greater economic engagement but also continued to view the threat of a hostile United States as a major national security concern (Goldstein, 2001).

Since the late 1980s, China has taken a more active interest in multilateralism, in part to deflect international suspicion and criticism of China's growing power. For instance, China signed the Comprehensive Test Ban Treaty in 1996 (although, like the United States, it has not ratified the treaty). China began to participate in UN Peacekeeping operations in 2000. It also cultivated the United States as a strategic partner, which led to both parties agreeing to establish a strategic partnership in 1997 (Goldstein, 2001). The United States championed China's accession to the World Trade Organization (WTO) thereafter, which was accomplished in 2001 (Prime, 2002). For the next decade, as China's economic growth soared, the U.S. and Chinese economies became more integrated with each other, as evidenced by trade and FDI data (U.S. Census Bureau, undated). Under the WTO agreement, China made significant concessions on FDI rules, allowing solely owned foreign enterprises to operate in a wide range of sectors for the first time. These rules have continued to be liberalized within, for example, banking, agriculture, and automobile sectors (Long, 2005). As a result, trade between the United States and China increased substantially, from a total volume of $200 billion per year (exports and imports) in 2001 to more than $730 billion in 2018 (including goods and services trade), falling to $635 billion in 2019, and rising again to $660 billion in 2020 (Office of the United States Trade Representative, undated).

In 2009, the United States and China initiated an annual strategic and economic dialogue. In those days, such neologisms as the "G-2" (i.e., the United States and China together designing and directing a new world order) and "Chimerica" were commonly heard, although Chinese officials rejected such descriptions (Lee, 2018). In July 2009, during a meeting with Chinese President Hu, President Obama noted that "the relationship between the United States and China will shape the 21st century, which makes it as important as any bilateral relationship in the world" (Obama, 2009). Earlier, in February 2009, then–Secretary of State Hillary Clinton, in advance of a visit to China during the global financial crisis, noted that although "some believe that China on the rise is, by definition, an adversary . . . we believe that the United States and China can benefit from and contribute to each other's successes" (Clinton, 2009).

The end of the Cold War thus necessitated a partial and successful change in China's grand strategy. The major change occurred within China's central goal, which shifted focus from survival to "rejuvenation" or regaining its historical status as a great power, enabled by its growing economic and military strength (Goldstein, 2020, p. 169).

Wang (2011) notes that what did not change with the end of the Cold War was China's focus on economic development. This focus has been constant since the end of the Cultural Revolution and the subsequent economic reforms introduced by Chinese leader Deng Xiaopeng in 1978 (Scobell et al., 2020, p. 11).

The development focus also increased China's interest in the Asia-Pacific. As a result of China's reliance on Asian supply chains for development since the early 1990s (bolstered by security concerns from U.S. actions in Asia), China's geostrategic focus was firmly focused on Asia and more so on Northeast and Southeast Asia during the first decade of the 21st century. The lack of focus on the rest of Asia was because countries of Central Asia and South Asia were poorly connected with China. Their economies were not as dynamic or forward-looking as those in Northeast and Southeast Asia, which limited their potential for China (Wang, 2011).

However, Chinese officials began to rethink their approach to the rest of Asia under Hu Jintao's leadership (2002–2012). Wang (2011, p. 78) notes that

> [t]he central government has been conducting the Grand Western Development Program in many western provinces and regions, notably Tibet and Xinjiang, for more than a decade. It is now more actively initiating and participating in new development projects in Afghanistan, India, Pakistan, Central Asia, and throughout the Caspian Sea region, all the way to Europe. This new western outlook may reshape China's geostrategic vision as well as the Eurasian landscape.

Preceding the Hu administration, Chinese leader Jiang Zemin (1989–2002) had promoted cooperation among China, Russia, and its Central Asian neighbors. The informal grouping that resulted, the Shanghai Five, achieved considerable success in resolving border disputes and reducing militarization along borders. The group was formalized as the SCO in 2001. According to Doshi (2021, p. 126), a key objective of China and Russia in promoting the SCO was to manage their rivalry with the United States.

The change in China's grand strategy from the period of the Cold War to the first two decades after the Cold War ended may be summarized as follows: (1) the focus of its main goal changed from survival to rejuvenation in order to build a pre-eminent Asian presence and a growing global presence in the socioeconomic, diplomatic, and defense arenas; (2) the objective of managing relations with the United States continued but with an expansion of China's strategies to include openness to trade relations, participation in multilateral institutions, and the formalization of the U.S.-China strategic partnership; (3) the objective of economic development continued but with a new plan to open China's doors to develop regional supply chains through trade openness; (3) a new objective to build political relations with Southeast and Northeast Asia to promote stable supply chains emerged; (4) a new objective to build security relations with Central Asia was implemented through the SCO, an institution promoted by China; and (5) the objective of building soft power in developing countries through participation in existing multilateral institutions continued.

Over the past decade, changing circumstances within and outside China have changed China's grand strategy. In 2012, when President Xi Jinping came into power, China faced several security challenges. Within Asia and Eurasia, China had successfully negotiated land border disputes with many countries. Taiwan's persistent autonomy remained an unresolved flash point, however, as did the disputed sections of the China-India border. There were and remain several maritime disputes in other parts of Asia with several ASEAN states over the South China Sea, with Japan over the East China Sea, and with the United States over the security of shipping lanes in the South China Sea and the Malacca Straits. Internally, terrorism in western China has been the biggest security challenge.

The most significant external security challenge came from the United States during the Trump administration. A hardening in the U.S. attitude toward China and its offshoots (i.e., the unexpected progress in the U.S.-Taiwan relationship and the social unrest in Hong Kong in 2019–2020) have added to China's security challenges.

It did not start that way. Chinese cooperation with U.S. initiatives concerning North Korean sanctions in the early years of the Trump administration promised a continuation of economic relations and the U.S.-China strategic partnership. This expectation was further bolstered by the Four Pillars relationship agreed to between the Trump and Xi administrations in 2017, covering (1) diplomatic and security issues, (2) economic issues, (3) law enforcement and cybersecurity, and (4) cultural and social issues (King, 2017; Lum, 2017).

Instead, since late 2017, there has been a dramatic reversal. The relationship between the United States and China transitioned from one of primarily market-based economic competition to one of escalating security competition and confrontation in many other domains, such as technology and diplomacy (Specialist in Asian Security Affairs, 2010; Dossani, 2020). The Trump administration, in December 2017, named China as a "strategic competitor" in its National Security Strategy document (Cordesman, 2017). A trade war, initiated by the United States in July 2018 and retaliated to by China, continues between the two countries. In October 2018, the United States named China as a reason for withdrawing from the Intermediate Range Nuclear Forces Treaty with Russia (Javed, 2018; U.S. Department of Defense, 2018). A January 2020 trade agreement between China and the United States focused on updating China's intellectual property regimes and committing China to purchasing more U.S. goods.

The United States now considers China to be its chief rival (Policy Planning Staff, Office of the Secretary of State, 2020). The Biden administration has named China as the United States' "most serious competitor," and foreign policy official Kurt Campbell noted that the "era of engagement with China [had] come to an end" (Zheng, 2021).

The present state of diplomatic dialogue between the United States and China is limited to bilateral initiatives, many of which appear to be failing.[1] Some observers argue that the

---

[1] Past and present bilateral initiatives between China and the United States include the following:

- U.S.-China Diplomatic and Security Dialogue (currently suspended)
- U.S.-China Law Enforcement and Cybersecurity Dialogue
- U.S.-China Comprehensive Economic Dialogue (currently suspended)

trend in China-U.S. relations is an inevitable outcome of the so-called Thucydides' trap (i.e., an environment characterized by increasing challenge and confrontation between an established and an emerging power) (Allison, 2017; Holmes, 2018). This environment suggests the possibility of a return to a cold war, but this time between the United States and China.

As of 2021, China's grand strategy may need to respond to the following list of U.S. concerns about China:

- Chinese assertiveness in the South China Sea, the Senkaku Islands, and the Taiwan Strait
- China's rising ability to compete with the United States economically; the unexpected economic growth of China from 2000 to 2010, averaging more than 10 percent per year, gave China unprecedented material power. As of 2021, China's savings rate, at 45 percent, is more than three times that of the United States while its GDP is 66 percent of the United States (CEIC Data, undated). As a result, China's total new investible capital annually is about twice that of the United States.
- China's unexpected and unprecedented economic integration with Northeast and Southeast Asia since 2000, as measured by the volume of total trade and supply-chain integration (Kwok and Koh, 2017); this raises economic security risks for the United States if China decides to withdraw from or otherwise constrict the supply chains, leading to shortages in goods imported by the United States.

Note the salience of Asia in the above U.S. concerns. Since the United States revamped its plans to compete with China, China has responded in the following ways. First, China has sought to "defend its core interests" (Goldstein, 2020, p. 179). One such response is to build its presence in disputed areas (Goldstein, 2020). For example, China has built military bases on reclaimed land in the South China Sea and criticized U.S. Freedom of Navigation operations there, breached Taiwan's air defense identification zone, and sent ships into the territorial waters of the Senkaku Islands.

Second, in the diplomatic sphere, as the United States has reduced or ended its involvement in key institutions, such as the UN and its agencies (e.g., Intergovernmental Panel on Climate Change [IPCC], World Health Organization [WHO]), the WTO, and the Trans-Pacific Partnership, China has sought greater engagement with those institutions. Within China, these are viewed as successful initiatives (Doshi, 2021, p. 109). This serves to "enhance China's own authority and reduce that of the United States within the broader institutional landscape over the longer term" (Ikenberry and Lim, 2017). As part of this strategy, Doshi (2021, p. 108) argues that China works through institutions to convince institutions' other members of China's "benign intentions" because it must abide by the institution's rules to be a member. This helps

---

- U.S.-China Strategic and Economic Dialogue (closed)
- U.S.-China Social and Cultural Dialogue
- China-U.S. Science and Technology Cooperation Agreement (closed)
- U.S.-China Human Rights Dialogue (currently suspended)
- U.S.-China Climate Change Dialogue (ongoing).

blunt U.S. power in such institutions, if the United States is a member, while building a hedge against a future downturn in China-U.S. relations. China's motives may also include the desire to weaken institutions in which the United States is a leading member (Doshi, 2021).[2]

Not all scholars agree that China's diplomatic strategy is primarily designed to address its rivalry with the United States. Taking a more benign view that China's diplomatic strategy is also intended to support its "good neighbor" objective, Scobell et al. (2020) states that "under the national rejuvenation grand strategy, China is rebalancing its diplomatic strategy to include not just maintaining good relations with the United States and other great powers but also enhancing ties with countries on China's periphery and across the developing world" (p. 37).

China's increased involvement in multilateral institutions is an expansion of China's long-standing commitment to multilateralism, particularly through the UN, for reasons that go beyond its own national security to project soft power. Since joining the UN and becoming a permanent member of its Security Council in 1971, China has been committed to the institution. One reason is that China has seen itself as the representative of the developing world in the Security Council. Over the past two decades, as its economic power has grown, China has used the UN as a vehicle to exercise soft power more widely. It is the second-largest contributor to the UN budget after the United States and a significant contributor to many of the UN's social welfare agencies (Ikenberry and Lim, 2017).

China's use of the veto in the Security Council in recent years reflects its rising ambitions for diplomatic power (see Figure 3.1). China's first veto after the Cold War was in 1997 and concerned human rights in Guatemala. More recently, most of China's vetoes concerned Syria, usually jointly with Russia and in opposition to the United States. It has also vetoed resolutions on Burma and Zimbabwe (UN, 2021).[3]

A third set of responses is in the socioeconomic sphere. First in importance to China is to continue to focus on its internal economic growth. Maintaining a high rate of economic growth builds material power relative to that of the United States, which is critical for managing China's more competitive rivalry with the United States. It also fulfills the key domestic objective of reinforcing the legitimacy of the regime. Material power is critical for "buttressing the nationalist narrative" of the Chinese Communist Party, promoted most recently by Xi Jinping in 2013, of the "China dream" of the "great rejuvenation of the Chinese nation" (quoted in Ikenberry and Lim, 2017).

High economic growth also helps China counter the United States by building soft power in the Asian developing world and beyond. In a 2014 speech, Xi Jinping noted that "the rise

---

[2] Doshi (2021, p. 103) argues that China has joined some institutions, such as the Asia Pacific Economic Cooperation forum in 1991, to weaken U.S. influence. However, it was not until the global financial crisis of 2007–2008 that China decided to promote its own institutions, reasoning that the United States was in decline as a global power and would not respond (Doshi, 2021, p. 213).

[3] Less obvious has been a reduction in the number of UN Security Council resolutions since 1992 because of China's prior stance that it would veto any resolution that it did not agree with.

FIGURE 3.1

Use of the Veto by Security Council Permanent Members from 1946 to Present

	1946–1969
	1970–1991
	1992–2021

China 16
France 16
United Kingdom 29
United States 82
Soviet Union/Russia 116

Number of vetoes cast

SOURCE: UN, 2021.

of its overall and national strength [gave] China the capability and the will to provide more public goods to the Asia-Pacific and the whole world" (Ikenberry and Lim, 2017).

Along with its increased involvement in multilateral institutions, China has also promoted or co-led new agreements and institutions, many with socioeconomic mandates that are focused on Asia (see Table 3.1). The Asia-specific initiatives include ASEAN+3 in 1999, the Brazil, Russia, India, China, and South Africa (BRICS) bank (now called the New Development Bank) in 2014 (Kondapalli, 2020), and the Regional Comprehensive Economic Partnership (RCEP) in 2020, all of which are targeted at economic growth. So is the Asian Infrastructure Investment Bank (AIIB), whose range of operations is primarily in Asia, but not exclusively so. As of 2021, the AIIB had 103 member countries compared with 68 members in the Asian Development Bank (ADB) and 119 members each in the World Bank and the International Monetary Fund.

An important channel for China's institutional socioeconomic initiatives is the trillion-dollar BRI, which was promoted by China in 2013. A global initiative, the BRI is implemented between governments on both a regional and bilateral basis, primarily to develop physical infrastructure, such as rail and pipelines. The National Development and Reform Commission (NDRC) of China manages the BRI under the guidance of the State Council. The NDRC determines, in consultation with partner countries, the projects to be undertaken; contracts out the projects to Chinese entities, most of which are state-owned banks and enterprises that are responsible for financing and implementation, including subcontracts to local entities; and monitors progress (Rolland, 2019).

While the BRI is officially described as a development initiative, it appears to fulfill two additional aims. The first is to increase other countries' economic dependence on China. This is because every corridor connects partner countries to China. An example is the China-Laos Railway, which is expected to connect the Laos economy closely with China's. The second aim is to secure Chinese access to critical locations: the markets of the west, the supply chains of Asia, and the mineral resources of the Middle East and Central Asia in the event of a maritime blockade. An example is the Kunming-Kyaukpyu Railway, which is under construction. Once the railway is completed, China will be able to bypass the Malacca Straits to send goods to its main markets and import mineral resources from its main suppliers.

One feature of China's socioeconomic initiatives is that, unlike its security or diplomatic initiatives, which have narrowly defined objectives, these are intended help fulfill plans that go beyond China's socioeconomic objectives. For example, the BRI, as noted above, addresses China's own development (a socioeconomic objective), the development of partner countries (a diplomatic aim of exercising soft power), economic interdependence with partner countries (a security objective), and securing access to critical locations (a security strategy). China may have taken this "one-arrow-many-targets" approach because it lacks enough breadth in its security and diplomatic initiatives to address all its security and diplomatic needs, and so must rely on socioeconomic objectives to address them.

Changes in China's Desired Outcomes

The above analysis suggests that China's goal for its grand strategy has not significantly changed over the decades since the Cold War ended. The focus of China's long-term goal is still rejuvenation—to regain China's standing as an advanced country and a great power.

However, China's desired outcomes have evolved in a few ways over the past decade and are now more interdependent with each other than they ever were. First, China's Asia focus covers all of Asia now, whereas, earlier, the emphasis was on only Southeast and Northeast Asia. This change is driven by China's economic needs, such as access to mineral resources, as well as security needs, such as securing its borders with Central Asian states.

A second change is that economic integration has replaced trade openness both for Asia and globally. This change is being accomplished primarily through outbound FDI, in which China now ranks as a world leader.

Third, because relations with the United States have changed to become more competitive, China needs to manage this rivalry instead of cultivating a strategic partnership.

Fourth, China seeks soft power engagement globally, whereas, earlier, this was targeted at the developing world.

Fifth, China's strategic toolkit relies increasingly on institutions—mainly socioeconomic institutions, but diplomatic and security institutions play a role as well.

Summary of China's Objectives and Plans

China currently looks to accomplish three outcomes: (1) achieve greater economic integration with Asia and the rest of the world, (2) manage its rivalry with the United States in Asia and globally, and (3) build soft power.

China's national plans to achieve its desired outcomes have also evolved over time. One of the main changes is China's increased use of institutions. From a survival-driven, largely noninstitutional approach during the Cold War, China has come to use institutions more actively (though not exclusively) thereafter to address the socioeconomic, diplomatic, and national security dimensions of China's interests. These institutions are multilateral, regional, and bilateral in nature and include both institutions that existed prior to China's involvement with them and new institutions, which over the past decade have been initiated or co-promoted by China, sometimes in competition with existing institutions.

Table 3.1 summarizes China's grand strategy as of 2021. China's national plans, as they appear in 2021, are as follows:

- economic plans
    - free trade agreements (FTAs), comprehensive economic partnerships
    - financial institutions
    - institutions and projects of the BRI

TABLE 3.1

China's Grand Strategy as of 2021

Goal	Desired Outcome (Type)	National Plan to Achieve Outcome	Most Prominent Example	Institutional Initiative (Yes/No)
Build a pre-eminent Asian presence and a larger global presence in the socioeconomic, diplomatic, and defense arenas	Increase economic integration with Asia and the world (economic)	1. FTAs, comprehensive economic partnerships 2. Financial institutions 3. BRI	1. RCEP (ASEAN) 2. AIIB 3. CPEC	1. Yes 2. Yes 3. Yes
	Manage rivalry with the United States in Asia and globally (security)	1. Bilateral and regional security associations 2. BRI 3. Defense of core interests through military action	1. SCO 2. Kunming-Kyaukpyu Railway 3. Military bases on reclaimed land in the South China Sea	1. Yes 2. Yes 3. No
	Build soft power engagement globally (diplomatic)	1. Multilateral and regional diplomacy associations 2. Defense of core interests through assertive diplomacy 3. Humanitarian aid 4. BRI	1. UN 2. Criticism of Taiwanese claims to sovereignty 3. WHO 4. China-Laos Railway	1. Yes 2. No 3. Yes 4. Yes

- security plans
  - bilateral and regional security associations
  - institutions and projects of the BRI
  - defense of core interests through military action
- diplomatic plans
  - multilateral and regional diplomacy associations
  - defense of core interests through assertive diplomacy
  - humanitarian aid
  - institutions and projects of the BRI.

China's institutional focus is clear. The economic strategies are the most comprehensive. Many are based on recently developed institutions, making it difficult to be definitive about their effectiveness. Table 3.2, which lists the institutions and initiatives promoted or co-promoted by China, illustrates the prominence of its socioeconomic strategies.

China's institutional security strategies, such as the SCO, have been successful; however, their use is limited in number and scope, causing China to use either noninstitutional strategies or economic strategies as alternatives to accomplish its security objective.

TABLE 3.2

Institutions and Initiatives Promoted or Co-Promoted by China Since 1999

Institution Name	Year of Establishment	Targeted Region	Targeted Outcome
ASEAN+3	1999	Southeast Asia	• Increase economic integration
AIIB	2016	All Asia	• Increase economic integration
BRI	2013	Global, but record shows focus on Asia	• Increase economic integration • Manage rivalry with the United States
Comprehensive Agreement on Investment	2020	Europe	• Increase economic integration • Manage rivalry with the United States
Forum on China-Africa Cooperation	2000	Africa	• Increase economic integration • Build soft power • Manage rivalry with the United States
New Development Bank	2014	Asia	• Increase economic integration
RCEP	2020	Northeast and Southeast Asia	• Increase economic integration • Manage rivalry with the United States
SCO	2001	Central Asia	• Manage rivalry with the United States

NOTE: This list excludes bilateral FTAs and bilateral strategic partnerships, which are also institutional initiatives.

The institutional diplomatic strategies have been quite successful with poor countries, but China's assertive diplomacy is less effective in China's periphery to the south and east, where China's vigorous defense of its core interests can be seen as coercive (Scobell et al., 2020, p. 43). This may be because China lacks an institutional mechanism for diplomatic and security purposes in Southeast and Northeast Asia. The contrast with its relations with Central Asian states, which are more stable and where China is not seen to be exercising coercive diplomacy, may be because there is no equivalent of the SCO for Southeast and Northeast Asia. Instead, China must use noninstitutional initiatives, with their attendant disadvantages when compared with institutional initiatives, or China must resort to using economic initiatives that were designed to fulfill its economic outcome to achieve diplomatic and security outcomes. Might this imply some gaps in China's grand strategy in achieving its security and diplomatic goals? To discuss China's Asia focus and the gaps that might exist in its grand strategy, we now turn to our interviews with subject-matter experts (SMEs).

Insights of Subject-Matter Experts

Our review of China's grand strategy in the first part of this chapter has revealed its strong emphasis on Asia to meet its three objectives (see Table 3.1). To help us understand which countries would be affected by China's grand strategy and how they might respond, we interviewed 22 former policymakers and policy analysts from China, Korea, other Asian countries, and the United States as part of our exploratory study. The sample selection procedure and representativeness are described in Appendix A.

We first asked SMEs to suggest the key multilateral and regional institutional and noninstitutional initiatives that China could use and the outcomes that China desired to accomplish with each initiative. This question, which we also addressed in the literature review, was supplemented by questions on bilateral initiatives. The results are shown in Table 3.3.

We then asked in which countries these initiatives were most important for China to have an effective grand strategy and the specific outcomes that China was seeking in these countries. The results are shown in Tables 3.4 and 3.5. We conclude this chapter with a discussion on China's use of institutions and their likely effectiveness.

SME assessments of multilateral and regional initiatives closely match the findings from our literature review (summarized in Table 3.1). The paramount significance of globalization in all respects to China's future is evident in the rankings shown in Table 3.3. The UN is, according to SMEs and consistent with our earlier discussion, China's main tool for intergovernmental multilateral initiatives. Lanteigne (2005) notes that China makes "active use of [the UN] institutions to promote the country's development of global power status." As one expert noted, the UN is an organization through which China has real influence .

The institutions and projects that constitute the BRI follow the UN in strategic importance to China among global institutions and initiatives. There are three reasons for the BRI's importance, according to SMEs. First is its scale. As a respondent noted, there is no conti-

TABLE 3.3

Key Institutional and Noninstitutional Initiatives Mapped to Outcomes Addressed

Rank	Importance of Initiative to Desired Outcome		
	Economic	Security	Diplomatic
Multilateral initiatives			
UN and its agencies	3	5	4
BRI	5	5	3
WTO	4.5	3	1
Regional initiatives			
ASEAN	4	4	3
SCO	3	4	5
Bilateral initiatives			
China-Russia Friendship Treaty	3	4	4
China-South Korea FTA	4	4	1
China-North Korea Friendship Treaty	2.25	4.5	5

NOTE: The ranking of initiatives shown in column 1 are from most- to least-important and represent the median score from SMEs' rankings of each. Importance of an initiative in relation to an outcome category (economic, security, diplomatic) is the median score of SMEs' rankings of each on a scale of 1 to 5, where 1 is least important and 5 is most important. To be included in this table, an initiative had to score a median rank of 4 or higher in at least one of the outcome categories. ASEAN includes SMEs who chose either RCEP or ASEAN+3.

nent that is not included under the BRI umbrella. Second, each BRI project tends to be large enough to affect the host country's growth prospects. Third, SMEs also noted that the transformative nature of the BRI for host countries not only strengthened China's own growth prospects but also opened opportunities for growth for many countries, especially in poorer regions. The potential impact on the economies of developing countries has helped bolster China's diplomatic standing among the governing elites of the same developing countries. Thus, not surprisingly, SMEs ranked the BRI highly for both developmental and diplomatic benefits to China.

The evidence suggests that the BRI receives a mixed reception from the public in host countries, many of whom question its financial benefits, the costs of debt incurred, and its effect on employment (Dossani, 2020). Official views tend to be more positive (China-Pakistan Economic Corridor Authority, undated; Walt, 2019). The literature suggests, though not conclusively, that the BRI-related projects have benefited host countries economically and diplomatically (Azhar and Syed, 2017; Rajah, Dayant, and Pryke, 2019; Brautigam, 2020).

WTO ranks third, primarily for the developmental benefits that it offers China. In the economic sphere, as the world's vendor of choice for manufactured goods, China has a particular stake in free trade. The WTO is a suitable organization for countries that support free trade, as China does, and China has benefited greatly from WTO membership.[4] Its attractiveness, despite the Trump administration's efforts to handicap it, is testimony to the advantages of the institutional approach, as discussed earlier.

In the security sphere, China has focused on regional institution-building, such as working with the ASEAN on a Code of Conduct and with the SCO. Its bilateral security arrangements have also been growing in number. SMEs widely noted the assertive behavior of China in recent years in Southeast and Northeast Asia, but they could not identify an institutional or noninstitutional initiative practiced by China that exemplified this issue.

Turning to bilateral relations, according to SMEs, Russia is China's most important partner. SMEs noted that because China and Russia share a common status of being adversaries of the United States, this has led the old foes to increase cooperation and coordination on multiple issues, despite persistent mutual suspicions. They are more likely to vote alike on the Security Council, as Figure 3.1 shows, than at any time in the past. They also work together in such regional bodies as the SCO and conclude bilateral economic deals, such as the China-Russia East gas pipeline.

Lukin's 2021 study of Sino-Russian relations compares two explanations for the two nations' growing relationship: (1) a marriage of convenience to counter the United States, and (2) convergent interests, values, and worldviews. He argues that the starting point for their closeness was indeed to counter the United States and dates to 2014, when Russia was removed from the Group of Eight, at the insistence of the United States, after Russia's annexation of Crimea. In 2015, the two countries agreed to merge the Russia-promoted Eurasian Economic Union with the BRI (Liu, 2019). When the United States named China as its strategic competitor in 2017, China sought even closer relations with Russia. Several current areas of cooperation are significant and strategic: They include Chinese investment in Russian technology, economic integration across Eurasia, cooperation in space, weapon sales by Russia to China, joint military exercises, and the creation of a missile attack warning system. Lukin (2021) concludes that the growing convergence of interests between China and Russia might have beneficial long-term effects on their relationship.

SMEs ranked the economic relationship between China and South Korea as China's second-most-important bilateral relationship. The FTA is important to both China and South Korea—China is South Korea's largest trading partner, and South Korea is China's third-largest trading partner (Kim, 2020).

The China-North Korea Friendship Treaty ranked third, ahead of other important relationships, such as the China-India relationship and the China-Japan relationship. SMEs

---

[4] Being a vendor (net exporter) economy rather than a client (net importer) nation can also impose constraints on China's strategy of institution-based free trade in that it must accept noninstitutional solutions when its counterparties have market power. This has been evident in China's response to U.S. restraints on trade under the Trump and Biden administrations. Rather than turn to the WTO after the United States launched its trade war on China in 2018, China responded to a U.S. request to negotiate a bilateral trade deal. Arguably, this may have had domestic benefits for China as well, because it led to the adoption of fairer trade and technology acquisition standards than those that China had adhered to earlier.

noted that this ranking reflects the deep-seated vulnerabilities on the Chinese side arising from concerns about North Korea's reliability as a partner, its regime's stability, its nuclear arsenal, and its economic dependence on China. The payoff for China is that this relationship increases China's diplomatic standing with South Korea and with the United States.

Interestingly, the U.S.-China trade deal of 2020 did not rank highly enough to be included among the list of bilateral initiatives. This may reflect the deal's reduced relevance under the Biden administration.

Having identified these key initiatives and their purposes, we sought to identify the countries where these initiatives would be used. For example, for managing rivalry with the United States, which initiatives would China use and where? We also sought more detail on the initiatives by asking the SMEs to comment on why these countries and initiatives were important for China. The results are shown in Tables 3.4 and 3.5.

The findings shown in Table 3.4 regarding the regions of importance are consistent with the findings of our literature review. Northeast Asia emerged as the most important region by a large margin. China's second- and third-largest trade partners, Japan and South Korea, are there. Both countries are allies of the United States, making China's relationships with each important to manage. China's relationship with Japan, with which China has disputes over territory in the East China Sea and which has been building up its military in recent years, is the more important of the two—perhaps because Japan is more committed to viewing China as an adversary than is South Korea. Japan also has closer economic and political relationships within Southeast Asia and South Asia (particularly with India) than does South Korea, and these are also regions of importance for China. Furthermore, Japan is a large investor in China and has transferred significant manufacturing technologies to China.

The third-most-important country to China in Northeast Asia is North Korea, for reasons discussed earlier concerning the China-North Korea Friendship Treaty. Taiwan makes a showing at only fourth place, a surprise considering the constant saber-rattling that characterizes China-Taiwan relations, the implications of failure for China on the legitimacy of the Chinese Communist Party, and Taiwan's close ties with the United States.

TABLE 3.4

Expert-Ranked Asian Regions and Countries of Importance to China

| Rank of Region | Region | Rank of Country Within Region | | | |
		1	2	3	4
1	Northeast Asia	Japan	South Korea	North Korea	Taiwan
2	Southeast Asia	Indonesia	Vietnam	Singapore	Thailand
3	South Asia	India	Pakistan	Sri Lanka	Bangladesh
4	Central Asia	Kazakhstan	Russia	Afghanistan	

NOTE: This table shows SMEs' responses to the request: "Please rank Asian regions and countries of interest in order of their importance to China." The ranking order of the regions and countries is based on SMEs' median score for each. We included entities that are not formally recognized as countries in SMEs' rankings of countries of importance to China.

Among regions, SMEs ranked Southeast Asia in second place. This is the region with which China is most economically integrated, particularly through supply-chain integration, trade, investment, and cultural exchanges. Furthermore, China's territorial claims in the South China Sea require China to manage its relations with countries in Southeast Asia carefully.

Kwok and Koh's 2017 study of economic integration of Southeast Asia with China shows how the rising role of agglomeration economies is increasing the importance of labor specialization. China is also playing an important role as the provider of FDI through business networks that include overseas Chinese citizens (Sargent, 2021).

Indonesia, despite its relatively passive stance in Southeast Asian affairs, ranks first, primarily on the grounds of its size and because it is actively engaging with China in the economic arena, more recently during the COVID-19 pandemic, and it has a large and influential Chinese population that is deeply economically engaged with China.

Vietnam ranks second, despite a complex, often adversarial relationship with China (Huy, 1998). Both are run by authoritarian, communist regimes. Vietnam is a recipient of large Chinese investments and counts China as its largest trading partner. On the other hand, the two countries have clashed in recent years over control of the Paracel Islands and hydrocarbon rights in the South China Sea, and Vietnam has growing defense ties with the United States.

Singapore's third-place showing reflects its outsize intellectual presence in the region. As one expert noted, it is the region's financial and logistics center and has always declared its openness to being a trusted intermediary between China and the United States, with which it has defense ties. Singapore has been an early investor in China, helping to develop industrial parks and other infrastructure.

Thailand's ranking, in fourth place, reflects the past and potential future rather than present reality. Just two decades ago, Thailand, with its economic dynamism, was seen as one of the most important partners of China. It has stagnated economically since, reducing its attractiveness to China. Because Thailand has an alliance with the United States, while being open to building relations with China, it is an important relationship to manage from China's perspective. The two countries have strong economic ties, and China is an important investor in Thailand via the BRI and other projects.

Turning to South Asia, which ranks third among the regions, India ranks in first place for several reasons. Its size and market potential are important for Chinese vendors, many of whom are large investors in India. From a diplomatic perspective, India has been open to close relations with China. This has changed in recent years for a variety of reasons, both domestic and geopolitical, and India has moved closer to the United States. India is an active participant with the United States, Australia, and Japan in the Quadrilateral Security Dialogue, which China views as an anti-China group. The border confrontations between China and India in Ladakh and Doklam over the past three years have significantly worsened relations, which led to India banning China from bidding for several large infrastructure projects. Despite these frictions, China-India trade relations are flourishing, and China is India's largest trading partner.

Pakistan ranks in second place for mostly positive reasons. China and Pakistan have a history of close relations, and China has sponsored the massive projects of the China-Pakistan Economic Corridor, which has already begun to transform Pakistan. Pakistan is a frontline state in the war against terrorism, which has the potential to destabilize China's Xinjiang province, while being a gateway for Chinese investment into Afghanistan. Pakistan's adversarial relationship with India offers China some tactical opportunities to confront India via Pakistan, while Pakistan's close military relationship with the United States requires careful management by China.

Sri Lanka, with its China-friendly government, strategic location in the Indian Ocean, and long-standing receipt of Chinese investment, ranks in third place. It is followed by Bangladesh, which is attractive to China for its growth potential, but the relationship needs more careful management, owing to Bangladesh's close relationship with India.

Central Asia ranks fourth as a region, driven in part by a continued lack of economic dynamism. However, its importance is likely to grow, given the stabilizing effect of the SCO and the growing trade and infrastructure links between China and Europe that pass through Central Asia (see, e.g., Beijing Trans Eurasia International Logistics, undated; European Commission, 2021). Of the Central Asian states, resource-rich Kazakhstan offers the most economic opportunity and is ranked first by SMEs, while Russia, which they ranked in second place, is important for strategic diplomatic and military reasons, as discussed earlier. Afghanistan, given the developments of 2021, is important for two reasons: (1) if it stabilizes, it will be an important destination for the BRI via Pakistan, but (2) it could be a source of instability in China's Xinjiang province if it remains unstable and looks to export terrorism.

Overall, it appears that China faces complex challenges in Asia. Although an analysis of China's relations with each country shown in Table 3.4 is outside the scope of this report, we provide an illustrative example of this complexity with a brief discussion of China-Vietnam relations. (We discuss country-specific challenges in greater detail in our case study of the Korean Peninsula in Chapter Four.)

As Vuving (2009) notes, "Within half a century, official definitions of the Sino-Vietnamese relationship traveled from 'comrades plus brothers' (1949–1977) to 'dangerous enemies' (1979–1988) to 'good neighbors, good friends, good partners, good comrades' (from 2002)." The support given by China to North Vietnam during its war with U.S.-supported South Vietnam held their relationship together, despite the Paracel Islands dispute of 1974, the China-Vietnam war of 1979, and the islands dispute of 1988. The subsequent territorial agreements of 1999 and 2000 were key turning points in the evolution of the Sino-Vietnamese relationship. Meanwhile, as in China, market reforms in Vietnam created a constituency that has favored economic integration with the capitalist Western world.

In 2005, signaling a new position of equidistance, Vietnam officially described the United States as a friend. Was this because the market integrationists' desire to sell to the lucrative American market overcame the anti-imperialist orientation of the Communist Party? Or was it a new threat to Beijing?

The more common view is that China's newfound assertiveness in the South China Sea under Xi Jinping is a threat to Vietnam (Le Thu, 2020). Under this view, Vietnam has improved its security through closer relations with the United States. However, this does not explain Vietnam's turn toward the United States in 2005.

In contrast, Vuving (2009) argues that the Iraq War played a key role in convincing the anti-imperialist camp that Vietnam might be next unless Vietnam developed closer relations with the United States in the security domain, as well as economic cooperation.

Vietnam is the subject of political overtures by the United States and may find it profitable to play off China and the United States. This is the case with India as well.

To summarize, as one expert noted, the countries of Asia, from a Chinese strategic perspective, can be sorted into three types:[5]

1. those that are already in the Chinese camp: Cambodia, Laos, Myanmar, Pakistan, and Sri Lanka
2. those that will never join the Chinese camp: Japan, Vietnam, India, and Australia
3. target countries for Chinese strategy: Indonesia, Malaysia, Thailand, and the Philippines.

The Southeast Asian countries within the Chinese camp lack resources, but several have important strategic locations. They also offer China the potential for supporting votes in ASEAN.[6] Sri Lanka, though more successful economically and strategically located in the Indian Ocean, is a small developing country.

The challenges of managing these complex relationships for China are twofold: (1) China does not have access to Asian allies with leverage, unlike the United States, and (2) China's grand strategy must address many more country-specific challenges than the U.S. strategy must.

Do the complexities of China's relations with the countries of Asia suggest that its grand strategy might not be up to the task? One particularly relevant case is of those Asian countries that China would like to influence with its strategies that are not yet within its camp (i.e., Indonesia, Malaysia, Singapore, South Korea, Thailand, and the Philippines). We examine this question more closely in Chapter Four.

We now turn to specific topics within each outcome category (economic, security, and diplomatic) to understand which institutional strategies China could develop and use to address them (see Table 3.5). We provided a list of topics (shown in column 1) to SMEs and asked them to rank the importance to China in working with different Asian countries for each topic on a scale of 1 (unimportant) to 5 (very important). Responses with a median rank

---

[5] Singapore would be categorized between types 2 and 3. South Korea also falls between these two types, but it is unlikely to ever join the Chinese camp.

[6] Myanmar's location could be of strategic value once the infrastructure to connect Kunming with Kyaukpyu is developed under several ongoing BRI projects.

TABLE 3.5

Experts' Mapping of China's Objectives to Asian Countries and China's Institutional Strategies

Objective	Key Asian Country	Institutional Strategy
Economic		
1. Trade and capital flows	• Japan • South Korea • ASEAN states	• WTO • RCEP • ASEAN-China FTA • China-ROK FTA
2. Intellectual property security	• Japan • South Korea	• WTO • RCEP
3. Facilities connectivity	• Kazakhstan • Pakistan • Thailand	• Institutions of the BRI
4. Financial integration	• Singapore • Japan • South Korea	• None available
5. Cybersecurity	• Japan • North Korea • Russia	• None available
Security		
1. Border security	• North Korea • Japan • India • Vietnam	• Mutual Friendship Treaty (with DPRK) • Comprehensive Strategic Partnership of Cooperation (with Vietnam)
2. Security of trade routes	• Indonesia • Japan • Philippines • Vietnam	• ASEAN Code of Conduct (under negotiation)
3. Homeland defense	• Taiwan • India • North Korea	• Mutual Friendship Treaty (with DPRK)
4. Policy coordination	• Japan • Indonesia • Russia	• China-Indonesia Comprehensive Strategic Partnership • Sino-Russian Treaty of Good-Neighborliness and Friendly Cooperation

Table 3.5—Continued

Objective	Key Asian Country	Institutional Strategy
Diplomatic		
1. Environmental protection	• India • Japan	• UN IPCC
2. Health security	• North Korea • Myanmar	• WHO • CIDCA
3. People-to-people exchanges	• South Korea • Japan • India	• Not available
4. Regime stability of partner country	• North Korea • Myanmar • Pakistan	• Mutual Friendship Treaty (with DPRK) • Comprehensive Strategic Cooperation Partnership (with Myanmar) • China-Pakistan Economic Corridor

NOTE: Countries listed in column 2 are in SME-ranked order and all received median ranking scores of 4 or higher on a 5-point scale (5 = very important).

of 4 or higher are shown in column 2. We also asked SMEs to comment on the strategies that China would use and whether they would involve institutions; their responses inform which strategies appear in column 3.

Table 3.5 shows that China would like to work with many countries in Asia to achieve its desired outcomes. Northeast and Southeast Asia are still the most important regions for all three outcome categories. China's institutional toolkit is mostly regional or multilateral for economic and diplomatic strategies. For security purposes, China relies significantly on bilateral strategic partnerships created over the past decade. These partnerships are underlain by agreements on the scope of the partnerships, the creation of working groups, and leadership summits. In this sense, such partnerships can be considered institutions, although they lack the formality of producing reports and joint statements, making assessments of their value difficult. The largest gap between outcomes and institutional strategies is with Japan. China's economy is already highly integrated with that of Japan, so it is possible that the recently formed RCEP will help China address multiple outcomes with Japan, but it is too early to tell.

In summary, both the literature and SMEs' insights have helped us identify China's main institutional and noninstitutional strategies to address its relations with key countries of Asia. The complex nature of relations with these countries suggests that China's increasing reliance on institutions may not always deliver its desired outcomes. To further explore this complexity, we turn to a case study of the countries of the Korean Peninsula.

CHAPTER FOUR

China's Grand Strategy and the Korean Peninsula

The Korean Peninsula is arguably a suitable test case of whether China's grand strategy, as articulated in Chapter Three, can be effective in all of Asia because of the following reasons:

- **Relevance to the target countries:** As shown in Table 3.5 in Chapter Three, all three outcome categories (economic, security, and diplomatic) of interest to China are of interest to North Korea and South Korea as well. In the case of North Korea, the overturning of sanctions by the UN is a priority that requires the cooperation of China (and the United States). North Korea needs humanitarian aid and economic development support, both of which China can provide. In the case of South Korea, it has seen its interest in closer ties with North Korea unrealized in part because of the United States' focus on North Korea's denuclearization, and South Korea may seek greater autonomy from the United States as a result (Snyder, 2018). This may drive South Korea to seek closer ties with China, a desire likely to be bolstered by the increasing interdependence of China and South Korea's economies, as well as their mutual interest to coordinate policy.

- **Relevance to China:** Both North Korea and South Korea are seeking to revise their relationships with China and the United States, thus creating opportunities and challenges for finding common ground with China. China has long regarded the U.S. military presence in South Korea as a potential threat and, therefore, finding ways to weaken Seoul's relationship with Washington could help erode the U.S. security presence. On the economic side, China would like to integrate its economy more closely with those of both North and South Korea, for reasons discussed below.

- **Generalizability of China's grand strategy:** China's grand strategy will not go unchallenged in the Korean Peninsula, just as it would not go unchallenged in most other Asian states. North Korea and South Korea will respond, as will external stakeholders, such as Japan and the United States. Furthermore, the Korean Peninsula, like each of the other Asian regions, has unique features which will likely require China to devise customized plans and strategies in response. How China does so in the Korean Peninsula could offer valuable lessons for the rest of Asia.

Our focus, therefore, is to identify which components of China's grand strategy have been implemented in the Korean Peninsula and any potential gaps in their effectiveness. This will allow us to draw conclusions about the likely effectiveness of China's grand strategy in the rest of Asia, which we discuss further in Chapter Five.

South Korea (also known as the Republic of Korea, ROK) and China established diplomatic ties in 1992. Mindful of the fact that the United States and South Korea are security allies, China focused on building a trade relationship with South Korea. However, China has also advanced itself as a competing leader for security issues on the peninsula through such efforts as the Six Party Talks.

Over the past decade, the Chinese and South Korean economies have integrated rapidly, particularly after the signing of a 2014 FTA. China holds South Korea's largest stock of FDI and is the largest destination for its exports.

Although the economic relationship with China is critical for South Korea, its relationship with North Korea is equally important—its management requires South Korea to be mindful of Chinese interests in North Korea.

South Korea is the smaller power in the relationship with China, which reduces its autonomy in developing policies toward China. There is a difference between small (and middle) powers and great powers in their level of autonomy in developing their grand strategies. The grand strategy of a small power must be set partly in response to a great power's grand strategy. This is because great powers can use their dominant status to impose their strategies on smaller countries. Of course, small powers may react by forming alliances among themselves to increase their collective power. In turn, great powers may preemptively create alliances with small powers. In both situations, small powers have less autonomy than great powers do.[1]

China's interests in North Korea (also known as the Democratic People's Republic of Korea, DPRK) are complex. The two countries signed a mutual defense pact in 1961, which until the time of this report's writing in 2021, was viewed by North Korea as playing some role in deterring Western interference in its affairs (Lo, 2021).[2] While careful to avoid destabilizing North Korea, Beijing was supportive of U.S. attempts to denuclearize North Korea

---

[1] An analogy to the economics literature is that big players can be market makers, while small players are always price takers.

Japan's quest for regional influence during the period 1960–1985, through infrastructure, trade, and aid strategies, is an example of a country seeking to exercise a high level of autonomy from the United States (while still maintaining their close security alliance). Japan's promotion of the ADB in 1966 after it failed to obtain an increased share in the World Bank—because of U.S. concerns—illustrates this. Although the United States was initially opposed to the ADB on the grounds that the World Bank was adequately funded, the United States later accepted the idea—and then worked with allies to ensure that Japanese influence over the ADB would be limited. This was accomplished primarily by locating the headquarters in Manila rather than, as expected by the Japanese, in Tokyo (ADB, 2017; Wan, 1995–1996).

[2] The two countries regularly reaffirm their ties under the treaty.

in the 1990s (Dumbaugh and Niksch, 2002).[3] China also chaired and hosted the Six Party Talks of 2003 to 2007 (Huang Ming, 2008). Under President Xi, China continued to support U.S. initiatives on North Korea through 2017. Driven by concerns about the effect of North Korean weaponization, both nuclear and ballistic, on its own security, China voted in favor of six Security Council resolutions sponsored by the United States to impose sanctions on North Korea between 2013 and 2017 (i.e., during both the Obama and Trump administrations) (Carnegie Endowment for International Peace, undated).

While Pyongyang's nuclear and missile tests threaten regional stability and are opposed by Beijing (Scobell et al., 2020), China has also often taken North Korea's side in confrontations with South Korea or when the United States has sought stricter sanctions and has always ensured that international sanctions do not threaten the survival of the Pyongyang regime (Albert, 2019). Chinese leaders fear that excessive sanctions may cause the Kim government to collapse, disrupting economic activity, sending thousands of refugees pouring into China's northeastern provinces, and bringing the South Korean military (and possibly its U.S. allies) to China's doorstep (Albert, 2019).

As shown in Table 3.4 in Chapter Three, SMEs recognize that China places great significance on its relations with North Korea. In terms of fitting in with China's developmental initiatives for the Chinese provinces that border DPRK (Jilin and Liaoning) and its hopes for bringing greater stability to the peninsula, North Korea plays an important role in China's diplomacy to countries in Northeast Asia (Cha, 2016; Silberstein, 2019).

China's strategies toward the two Korean countries are likely to be more effective when the underlying objectives are similar and less effective otherwise. We discussed objectives of China and the two Korean countries vis-à-vis each other with SMEs, and their views on mutual objectives are summarized in Table 4.1.

As shown in Table 4.1, China and South Korea share two interests for North Korea: regime stability and enhancing trade and capital flows. On the first, regime stability, both worry about the consequences of regime collapse, including refugee flows and control over North Korea's nuclear arsenal. China's strategy regarding regime stability in North Korea is to provide economic support and humanitarian aid and, through their mutual friendship treaty, provide assurances about long-term diplomatic and military support.

On the second objective, trade and capital flows, most SMEs said that North Korea would welcome investments from China and South Korea, provided that the type of investment was appropriate. North Korea also seeks help from China and South Korea to lessen the effects of international sanctions. Investments, such as those in foreign-owned industries, would be concerning to North Korea if they were accompanied by large expatriate populations. This would expose ordinary North Koreans to expatriate wealth and lifestyles, which would be unacceptable to the DPRK leadership. On the other hand, such investments as power lines

---

[3] Beijing was less helpful than the United States would have liked. That being said, Beijing clearly did not seek a leadership role on the issue, nor did it seem to be directly attempting to undermine U.S. leadership, although its insistence on keeping the North Korean state marginally viable may have had that effect.

TABLE 4.1

Mutual Objectives Among China, North Korea, and South Korea

China's Objectives	North Korea's Objectives	South Korea's Objectives
For North Korea	For China	For North Korea
Regime stability	Capital flows (inbound FDI)	Regime stability
Border security	Border security	People-to-people exchange
Trade and capital flows (including facilities connectivity)	Policy coordination (regarding sanctions)	Trade and capital flows (including facilities connectivity)
For South Korea	For South Korea	For China
Trade and capital flows	Border security	Trade and capital flows
Homeland defense	Capital flows (inbound FDI)	Homeland defense
Policy coordination (regarding the ROK-U.S. alliance)		Policy coordination (regarding North Korea)

NOTE: SMEs were asked to select objectives from a list with the option to add their own. This table shows their top-ranked objectives. For the full list of objectives of China's grand strategy, see column 1 of Table 3.5.

and other infrastructure that could be built with foreign funding, with limited long-term foreign involvement, and handed over to North Korean management, would be welcomed by the DPRK. The BRI, which focuses on infrastructure development, and to which both North Korea and South Korea (since 2018) belong, would be an appropriate vehicle. China, which is looking to BRI projects to bring development to its northeastern provinces, would welcome this, too. Of course, the current sanctions regime imposed by the Security Council rules out these investments for the moment.

In 2013, the Park Geun-hey government of South Korea announced a "Eurasia Initiative," with the intention of building infrastructure, transportation, and energy in the north of South Korea, potentially jointly with the BRI. The Moon Jae-in government, which has repeatedly called for a "peace regime" for the Korean Peninsula, pursues a similar but modified initiative called New Northern Policy, which emphasizes the importance of strengthening ties with Russia, China, Mongolia, and other Central Asian countries. Chinese entities have also expressed interest. For example, in 2018, the province of Liaoning proposed a rail system that links the city of Dandong in China to Pyongyang in North Korea and to Seoul and Busan in South Korea, as well as a new road between Dandong and Pyongyang through Sinuiju, a North Korean city (Zhou, 2018).

Some SMEs noted that, although South Korea is a member of the BRI, it will weigh the impact of its participation in that initiative against its alliance with the United States. Although the ROK-U.S. alliance does not impose any constraints on the ROK's economic freedoms, the current era of China-U.S. rivalry may lead the ROK to take a cautious approach to co-investing with China through the BRI.

China and South Korea are aligned on trade and investment as their top mutual priority. The ROK-China FTA and the WTO are adequate mechanisms to deal with these under normal circumstances. During the Trump administration, the South Korean government faced pressure from the United States to reduce its reliance on China-centric supply chains. Under the Biden administration, this pressure may have reduced—there being no mention of China in the Biden-Moon joint statement after their meeting in May 2021 (White House, 2021).

Homeland defense is a common concern that both China and South Korea have with regard to each other, but for different reasons. China's concern arises from the U.S.-ROK alliance. Early in the Moon Jae-in administration, controversy erupted over Chinese opposition to South Korea's deployment of the U.S. Terminal High Altitude Area Defense (THAAD) missile defense system, which Beijing claimed threatened its own security by allowing the United States to monitor its northeast provinces and Central China with THAAD's radar. China responded by leveling major sanctions against South Korea, although both sides were able to resolve the issue in 2017 when South Korea agreed not to build a trilateral missile shield, ally itself with Japan and the United States, or deploy additional THAAD batteries (Allen et al., 2019).

South Korea's concern arises from the threat of North Korea's use of nuclear weapons in a confrontation with South Korea. According to SMEs, the priorities for South Korea to deal with this threat are to support the DPRK's economy, encourage people-to-people exchanges with the DPRK, and help stabilize its regime. These three policies were preferred to efforts to eliminate the DPRK's nuclear arsenal or address the (significant) threat of an artillery attack from the DPRK side of the demilitarized zone on Seoul (Gentile et al., 2019). This view may be because denuclearization is not seen as a realistic goal. Furthermore, South Korea is building up its conventional deterrence capabilities to address the threat of an artillery attack (Bowers and Hiim, 2020/21).

The two countries' third common priority is the need for policy coordination. South Korea would like more coordination with China on the nuclear threat from North Korea—although this assumes that China is informed about the threat and can do something about it. For China, policy coordination is important in two areas: (1) preventing a recurrence of issues arising from the U.S.-ROK alliance, such as the THAAD issue; and (2) ensuring that trade and investment between the two countries is not subject to U.S. pressure on South Korea, such as it faced during both the Trump and Biden administrations on limiting its semiconductor exports to China (Global Times, 2021).

In summary, China and South Korea share two common interests for and with North Korea: regime stability and enhancing trade and capital flows. They are aligned on trade and investment as their top mutual priority. And homeland defense is a common concern that both countries have with regard to each other, but for different reasons. China's concern arises from the U.S.-ROK alliance. South Korea's concern arises from North Korea's nuclear and conventional weapons threat to South Korea, on which, it believes, China can play a helpful role to mitigate.

Both China and North Korea share a concern about mutual border security. China's concern arises from the risk of refugee flows in the event of a political or humanitarian crisis in

North Korea, while North Korea is concerned about illegal migration of skilled labor (including defectors) across the border.

China's institutional strategies are likely to be more effective when its interests are aligned with those of its partner countries than when interests or their underlying causes differ, because it is then more likely that the partner country will agree to the institution's standards and rules. For example, the common economic interests in trade, capital flows, and facilities connectivity across the three countries suggest that China's strategies for economic integration through the BRI could be effective. Similarly, regime stability of North Korea is a common interest, suggesting that China's strategies, which are, as discussed above, to provide economic support and humanitarian aid and, through their mutual friendship treaty, to provide assurances about long-term diplomatic and military support, could also be effective.

However, because interests differ among countries as well, institutional strategies may not always be successful (see Table 4.2).

Table 4.2 shows how China's institutional strategies can be effective in both North and South Korea. Trade and capital flows through the BRI for both countries and, for South Korea, the China-ROK FTA and RCEP are increasingly likely to be the key drivers of China's relations with it.

Table 4.2 also shows some limitations in China's use of institutions as part of its grand strategy. In the important areas of homeland defense and policy coordination with South Korea, China is reliant on bilateral negotiations because there is currently no institutional option at hand.[4] The weakness of the Chinese approach was evident when it objected to South Korea's deployment of the U.S. THAAD missile defense system. Because South Korea's assurances were in line with existing South Korean policy, the resolution appears to be mostly a face-saving move by China—the original THAAD system remains in place.

South Korea, caught as it is between the economic benefits of a close relationship with China and the security benefits of the U.S.-ROK alliance, has no easy way to respond to China's grand strategy in the context of growing U.S.-China rivalry. South Korea could diversify its economic relations away from China, but it seems to have decided not to do so, as its membership in RCEP indicates. It could consider new alliances, perhaps within Northeast Asia, Southeast Asia, or South Asia. However, South Korea's historically difficult relations with Japan seem to rule out the possibility of a Northeast Asian option. Southeast Asia contains states that have surmounted hurdles in their relationships with China, such as the Philippines and Vietnam, but these countries' economic interdependence with China might rule out an alliance with South Korea. In South Asia, India is a possibility, given its great-power ambitions and limited economic integration with China. However, India, given its long land border with China, which has recently been subject to low-intensity conflict, is likely to be extremely cautious about provoking China with an alliance with a middle power of limited value to India.

---

[4] The now-defunct Six Party Talks provided China with an institutional channel for policy coordination with South Korea and the other participants.

TABLE 4.2

China's Grand Strategy for the Korean Peninsula

China's Objectives	China's Strategies	Use of Institutions
Priorities for North Korea		
Regime stability	1. Mutual friendship treaty 2. Aid	Yes No
Border security	1. Mutual friendship treaty	Yes
Trade and capital flows (including facilities connectivity)	1. Institutions of the BRI	Yes
Priorities for South Korea		
Trade and capital flows	1. China-ROK FTA and RCEP 2. WTO 3. Institutions of the BRI	Yes
Homeland defense	1. Bilateral negotiations	No
Policy coordination	1. Bilateral negotiations	No

NOTE: The SME-ranked objectives shown in column 1 replicate those shown in Table 4.1. The strategies in column 2 are shown from most- to least-important based on the SMEs' ranking of a list of China's strategies.

The United States will likely be an active player as well. It has encouraged South Korea to invest more in the United States, reduce technology cooperation with China, and diversify its economy away from China-centered supply chains. On the diplomatic side, the United States has emphasized its commonality of values with South Korea, and on the security side, the United States and South Korea have jointly reaffirmed the durability of their alliance. It is not clear whether these approaches will succeed, given that the alliance, from a South Korean viewpoint, does not target China, while the low costs and skills in China make economic integration with it attractive for South Korea. Taiwan offers a cautionary tale: Despite having the political will to economically "decouple" from China, it has not succeeded in doing so after more than half a decade of efforts. Why would South Korea?

CHAPTER FIVE

Concluding Discussion

In this report, we have provided our understanding of China's grand strategy and its implications for Asia, drawing on the results of our literature review and interviews with SMEs. Our analysis suggests that China's grand strategy, as it appears in 2021, may be stated as follows: The long-term goal of China's grand strategy is to build a pre-eminent Asian presence and a growing global presence in the socioeconomic, diplomatic, and military arenas. To achieve this goal, China currently desires to accomplish three outcomes: (1) increase economic integration with Asia and the rest of the world, (2) manage its rivalry with the United States, and (3) build soft power globally.

The national plans to achieve China's desired outcomes, as they appear in 2021, are increasingly institutional and are as follows:

- economic plans
  - FTAs, comprehensive economic partnerships
  - financial institutions
  - institutions and projects of the BRI
- security plans
  - bilateral and regional security associations
  - institutions and projects of the BRI
  - defense of core interests through military action
- diplomatic plans
  - multilateral and regional diplomacy associations
  - defense of core interests through assertive diplomacy
  - humanitarian aid
  - institutions and projects of the BRI.

China increasingly relies on multilateral, regional, and bilateral institutions to achieve its objectives. These institutions include those that existed prior to China's involvement with them and new institutions. The latter group includes institutions that China has initiated or co-promoted—sometimes in competition with existing institutions.

China's institutional security strategies, such as the SCO, have been successful; however, their use is limited in number and scope, causing China to either use noninstitutional strategies or economic strategies as alternatives to accomplish its security objective.

China's institutional diplomatic strategies have been quite successful with poor countries around the world, but China has been practicing an assertive form of diplomacy in China's periphery to its south and east that can be seen as coercive. This may be because China lacks an institutional mechanism for diplomatic and security purposes in Southeast and Northeast Asia. The contrast with its relations with Central Asian states, which are more stable and where China is not seen to be exercising coercive diplomacy, may be because there is no equivalent of the SCO for Southeast and Northeast Asia. Instead, China must use noninstitutional initiatives, with their attendant disadvantages when compared with institutional initiatives, or China must resort to using economic initiatives that were designed to fulfill its economic outcome to achieve its diplomatic and security outcomes.

To help understand which countries within Asia would be affected by China's grand strategy and how they might respond, we interviewed subject-matter experts from China, Korea, other Asian countries, and the United States. Our analysis of Asian countries of interest to China suggests the following conclusions:

- China would like to work with a large number of countries in Asia to achieve its desired outcomes. Northeast and Southeast Asia are still the most important regions for all three outcome categories.
- China's institutional toolkit includes mostly regional or multilateral institutions for economic and diplomatic purposes. For security purposes, China relies significantly on bilateral institutions, typically strategic partnerships created over the past decade.
- The complex nature of China's relations with key countries suggests that China's increasing reliance on institutions may not always deliver its desired outcomes. The largest gap between outcomes and institutional strategies is with Japan. China's economy is already highly integrated with Japan's, so it is possible that the recently formed RCEP will help China address multiple outcomes with Japan, but it is too early to tell.

To further explore this complexity, we examined China's relations with the countries of the Korean Peninsula. Our review of the three countries' mutual interests showed that China and South Korea share two common interests for and with North Korea: regime stability and enhancing trade and capital flows. China and South Korea are also aligned on trade and investment as their top mutual priority.

Homeland defense is a common concern that China and South Korea face with regard to each other, but for different reasons. China's concern arises from the U.S.-ROK alliance. South Korea's concern arises from North Korea's nuclear and conventional weapons threat to South Korea, which, it believes, China can play a helpful role to mitigate.

Both China and North Korea share a concern about border security. China's concern arises from the risk of refugee flows in the event of a political or humanitarian crisis in North Korea, while North Korea is concerned about the illegal migration of skilled laborers (including defectors) across the border.

Despite the many common interests that China shares with both North and South Korea, China's grand strategy is likely to face challenges, in large part because of the absence of adequate institutional mechanisms to deal with them.

For middle Asian powers like South Korea, China's grand strategy raises important issues, given China's ambitions, economic power, and economic interdependence with Asia. These issues require such countries to choose between working with Chinese economic institutions or diversifying their economies to be less dependent on China and between accepting Chinese primacy in addressing their security needs or building their own coalitions.

China's arrival on the world stage in recent years requires other powers, great and small, to respond to China's grand strategy. The countries of Asia are mostly middle powers like South Korea, with uniquely complex relations with great powers that make a simple response difficult. As the great powers execute their grand strategies, small and middle powers may bear a considerable share of the fallout.

Subject-Matter Expert Sample Description

We interviewed 22 former policymakers and current policy analysts from China (4), South Korea (5), other Asian countries (5), and the United States (8). The sample is further described in Table A.1.

Our sample was, by design, limited to senior policy analysts with at least ten years of relevant experience and high-level former policymakers—at minimum, they were former ambassadors to an Asian country. We did include, however, one former policymaker who held a position lower than ambassador on the grounds that the person concerned had traveled several times to North Korea as a diplomat and could provide a sense of DPRK thinking. We also included one policy analyst from the "Other Asian countries" category who had less than ten years of relevant experience for the purpose of increasing country diversity.

The policy analysts were selected from a list derived from the literature of senior academics in the field.

Our sampling methodology is non-random and biased, but the sample that we have selected is intended to include representatives of the underlying population, which makes it a valid form of sampling for this exploratory qualitative analysis.

TABLE A.1

Subject-Matter Expert Characteristics

Country or Region	Former Policymaker	Policy Analyst	Total
China	0	4	4
South Korea	1	4	5
Other Asian countries	3	2	5
United States	1	7	8
Total	5	17	22

Glossary

Desired outcome	A component of a nation's *grand strategy*; used interchangeably with *objective*, this refers to a specific long-term national target whose accomplishment contributes to achieving the nation's goals
Economic integration	The removal of barriers to trade in goods and services and the free movement of capital and technology
Goal	A component of a nation's *grand strategy*, this refers to a statement of the nation's vision of what it aspires to become
Grand strategy	A statement that specifies national goals, objectives, and implementation plans; its components are *goals*, *desired outcomes* or *objectives*, and *instruments*, *plans*, *strategies*, and *toolkits*
Instrument	A component of a nation's grand strategy; used interchangeably with *plan*, *strategy*, and *toolkit*, this refers to the long-term national plan whose implementation contributes to achieving a *desired outcome* or *objective*
Objective	A component of a nation's *grand strategy*; used interchangeably with *desired outcome*, this refers to a specific long-term national target whose accomplishment contributes to achieving a national *goal*
Plan	A component of a nation's *grand strategy*; used interchangeably with *instrument*, *strategy*, and *toolkit*, its implementation contributes to achieving a *desired outcome* or *objective*
Soft power	The ability to shape external perceptions about a country's policies through noncoercive methods; the instruments of soft power include cultural exchanges, public diplomacy, foreign aid, and technical cooperation

Strategy

Different from *grand strategy,* this is a component of a nation's *grand strategy*; used interchangeably with *instrument, plan,* and *toolkit,* this refers to the long-term national plan whose implementation contributes to achieving a *desired outcome* or *objective*

Toolkit

A component of a nation's *grand strategy*; used interchangeably with *instrument, plan,* and *strategy,* this refers to the long-term national plan whose implementation contributes to achieving a *desired outcome* or *objective*

Abbreviations

ADB	Asian Development Bank
AIIB	Asian Infrastructure Investment Bank
ANZUS	Australia, New Zealand, United States Security Treaty
ASEAN	Association of Southeast Asian Nations
BRI	Belt and Road Initiative
CIDCA	China International Development and Cooperation Agency
CPEC	China-Pakistan Economic Corridor
DPRK	Democratic People's Republic of Korea (North Korea)
FDI	foreign direct investment
FTA	free trade agreement
IMF	International Monetary Fund
IPCC	Intergovernmental Panel on Climate Change
NATO	North Atlantic Treaty Organization
RCEP	Regional Comprehensive Economic Partnership
ROK	Republic of Korea (South Korea)
SCO	Shanghai Cooperation Organisation
SME	subject-matter expert
THAAD	Terminal High Altitude Area Defense
UN	United Nations
WB	World Bank
WHO	World Health Organization
WTO	World Trade Organization

References

ADB—*See* Asian Development Bank.

Al-Qahtani, Mutlaq, "The Shanghai Cooperation Organization and the Law of International Organizations," *Chinese Journal of International Law*, Vol. 5, No. 1, March 2006, pp. 129–147.

Albert, Eleanor, "The China–North Korea Relationship," Council on Foreign Relations, June 25, 2019.

Allen, Gregory, Allison Astorino-Courtois, Michael Beckley, Belinda Bragg, L. R. Bremseth, Dean Cheng, Skye Cooley, Dale Copeland, Joseph DeFranco, David R. Dorondo, Anoush Ehteshami, Daniel J. Flynn, Chistopher D. Forrest, James Giordano, E. J. Gregory, Robert Hinck, Maorong Jiang, Michael Mazarr, Eric McGlinchey, Girish Nandakumar, Cynthia Roberts, John Schurtz, Thomas Sherlock, Robert Spalding III, Cynthia Watson, Richard Weitz, Nicholas D. Wright, Nicole Peterson, and Sabrina Pagano, *Chinese Strategic Intentions: A Deep Dive into China's Worldwide Activities*, Boston: NSI, December 16, 2019.

Allison, Graham, *Destined for War: Can America and China Escape Thucydides's Trap?* New York: Houghton Mifflin Harcourt, 2017.

ASEAN—*See* Association of Southeast Asian Nations.

Asian Development Bank, *ADB Through the Decades: ADB's First Decade (1966–1976)*, Manila, Philippines, September 2017.

Association of Southeast Asian Nations, "About ASEAN," webpage, undated. As of September 1, 2021:
https://asean.org/about-us

Atlantic Council, "About the Atlantic Council," webpage, undated. As of September 1, 2021:
https://www.atlanticcouncil.org/about/

Azhar, Harris, and Amna Syed, *Impact of China-Pakistan Economic Corridor (CPEC) on the Energy Sector of Pakistan*, Vol. 3, *Corridors, Culture, and Connectivity*, Islamabad, Pakistan: Pakistan-China Institute, October 2017.

Beijing Trans Eurasia International Logistics, website, undated. As of November 7, 2021:
http://en.trans-eurasia.com/

Bowers, Ian, and Henrik Stålhane Hiim, "Conventional Counterforce Dilemmas: South Korea's Deterrence Strategy and Stability on the Korean Peninsula," *International Security*, Vol. 45, No. 3, Winter 2020/21, pp. 7–39.

Brautigam, Deborah, "A Critical Look at Chinese 'Debt-Trap Diplomacy': The Rise of a Meme," *Area Development and Policy*, Vol. 5, No. 1, 2020, pp. 1–14.

Carnegie Endowment for International Peace, "Making Sense of UN Sanctions on North Korea," undated. As of September 1, 2021:
https://carnegieendowment.org/publications/interactive/north-korea-sanctions

CEIC Data, "China Gross Savings Rate," webpage, undated. As of September 20, 2021:
https://www.ceicdata.com/en/indicator/china/gross-savings-rate

Cha, Victor D., "The North Korea Question," *Asian Survey*, Vol. 56, No. 2, March/April 2016, pp. 243–269.

China-Pakistan Economic Corridor Authority, "About CPEC: Introduction," webpage, undated. As of September 6, 2021:
http://cpec.gov.pk/introduction/1

China International Development Cooperation Agency, "What We Do," webpage, August 1, 2021. As of September 5, 2021:
http://en.cidca.gov.cn/2018-08/01/c_259525.htm

CIDCA—*See* China International Development Cooperation Agency.

Clinton, Hillary Rodham, "U.S.-Asia Relations: Indispensable to Our Future," transcript of remarks at the Asia Society, New York, February 13, 2009. As of November 7, 2021:
https://2009-2017.state.gov/secretary/20092013clinton/rm/2009a/02/117333.htm

Cordesman, Anthony H., "President Trump's New National Security Strategy," Center for Strategic & International Studies, December 18, 2017.

Doshi, Rush, *The Long Game: China's Grand Strategy to Displace American Order*, Cambridge, United Kingdom: Oxford University Press, 2021.

Dossani, Rafiq, *Engagement with North Korea: A Portfolio-Based Approach to Diplomacy*, Santa Monica, Calif.: RAND Corporation, RR-A432-1, 2020. As of August 1, 2021:
https://www.rand.org/pubs/research_reports/RRA432-1.html

Dumbaugh, Kerry, and Larry Niksch, *Sino-U.S. Summit, October 2002*, Washington, D.C.: Congressional Research Service, RS21351, November 6, 2002.

European Commission, "EU-China Comprehensive Agreement on Investment: Milestones and Documents," webpage, July 26, 2021. As of November 7, 2021:
https://trade.ec.europa.eu/doclib/press/index.cfm?id=2115

Freeman, Chas W., Jr., "The United States and China: Game of Superpowers," Remarks to the National War College Student Body, Fort Lesley J. McNair, Washington, D.C., February 8, 2018. As of September 1, 2021:
https://chasfreeman.net/the-united-states-and-china-game-of-superpowers/

———, "China's National Experiences and the Evolution of PRC Grand Strategy," in David Shambaugh, ed., *China and the World*, Oxford, United Kingdom: Oxford University Press, 2020, pp. 37–60.

G7 UK, "What is the G7?" webpage, undated. As of September 1, 2021:
https://www.g7uk.org/what-is-the-g7/

Gentile, Gian, Yvonne K. Crane, Dan Madden, Timothy M. Bonds, Bruce W. Bennett, Michael J. Mazarr, and Andrew Scobell, *Four Problems on the Korean Peninsula: North Korea's Expanding Nuclear Capabilities Drive a Complex Set of Problems*, Santa Monica, Calif.: RAND Corporation, TL-271-A, 2019. As of August 1, 2021:
https://www.rand.org/pubs/tools/TL271.html

Global Times, "US Might Force Samsung to Restrict Exports to China, but Complete Decoupling Unlikely," May 21, 2021. As of September 6, 2021:
https://www.globaltimes.cn/page/202105/1224121.shtml

Goldstein, Avery, "The Diplomatic Face of China's Grand Strategy: A Rising Power's Emerging Choice," *China Quarterly*, Vol. 168, December 2001, pp. 835–864.

———, "China's Grand Strategy Under Xi Jinping: Reassurance, Reform, and Resistance," *International Security*, Vol. 45, No. 1, Summer 2020, pp. 164–201.

Hart, B. H. Liddell, *Strategy*, New York: Praeger, 1967.

Holmes, James, "Can America and China Avoid the Pull of the Thucydides Trap?" *National Interest*, October 19, 2018.

Huang Ming, "China's Ministry of Foreign Affairs on the Six-Party Talks, China-France Relations, etc. (Factual Record)" [中国外交部就六方会谈、中法关系等(实录)_资讯_凤凰网], China News, December 16, 2008. As of September 6, 2021: https://news.ifeng.com/mainland/200812/1216_17_924803.shtml

Huy, Nguyen Ngoc, "The Confucian Incursion into Vietnam," in Walter H. Slote and George A. De Vos, eds., *Confucianism and the Family*, Albany, N.Y.: SUNY Press, July 1998, pp. 91–104.

Ikenberry, G. John, and Darren Lim, *China's Emerging Institutional Statecraft—The Asian Infrastructure Investment Bank and the Prospects for Counter-Hegemony*, Washington, D.C.: Brookings Institute, April 2017.

Javed, Saman, "Trump Withdrawal from Missile Treaty Could Escalate US Tensions with China, Experts Warn," *The Independent*, October 23, 2018.

Johnston, Alastair Iain, *Social States*, Princeton, N.J.: Princeton University Press, 2014.

Kastner, Scott L., Margaret M. Pearson, and Chad Rector, *China's Strategic Multilateralism: Investing in Global Governance*, Cambridge, United Kingdom: Cambridge University Press, 2018.

Kennedy, Paul, *Grand Strategies in War and Peace*, New Haven, Conn.: Yale University Press, 1991.

Kim, Victoria, "When China and U.S. Spar, It's South Korea That Gets Punched," *Los Angeles Times*, November 19, 2020.

King, Nathan, "US-China Comprehensive Dialogue and Its Four Pillars," CGTN America, November 7, 2017.

Kondapalli, Srikanth, "Regional Multilateralism with Chinese Characteristics," in David Shambaugh, ed., *China and the World*, Oxford, United Kingdom: Oxford University Press, 2020, pp. 313–340.

Kraus, Charles, "The Sino-Soviet Alliance, 70 Years Later," Wilson Center, February 12, 2020.

Kwok, Andrei O. J., and Sharon G. M. Koh, "Economic Integration in Southeast Asia: Its Impact on the Business Environment," *Journal of International Business Education,* Vol. 12, 2017, pp. 309–320.

Lanteigne, Marc, *China and International Institutions: Alternate Paths to Global Power*, London: Routledge, 2005.

Le Thu, Huong, "Rough Waters Ahead for Vietnam-China Relations," Carnegie Endowment for International Peace, September 30, 2020.

Lee, John, "Killing Chimerica," *The Interpreter,* October 19, 2018.

Liu, Xin, "What Makes Russia an Important Player in BRI?" *The Point*, May 1, 2019.

Lo, Kinling, "China, North Korea Reaffirm Ties on Defence Treaty Anniversary," *South China Morning Post*, July 11, 2021.

Long, Guoqiang, "China's Policies on FDI: Review and Evaluation," in Theodore H. Moran, Edward M. Graham, and Magnus Blomström, eds., *Does Foreign Direct Investment Promote Development?* Washington, D.C.: Institute for International Economics, Center for Global Development, April 2005, pp. 315–336.

Lukin, Alexander, "Have We Passed the Peak of Sino-Russian Rapprochement?" *Washington Quarterly*, Vol. 44, No. 3, 2021, pp. 155–173.

Lum, Thomas, *Human Rights in China and U.S. Policy: Issues for the 115th Congress*, Washington, D.C.: Congressional Research Service, July 17, 2017.

Makinda, Samuel M., "Sovereignty and International Security: Challenges for the United Nations," *Global Governance*, Vol. 2, No. 2, 1996, pp. 149–168.

Ministry of Foreign Affairs of the People's Republic of China, "President Xi Jinping Delivers Important Speech and Proposes to Build a Silk Road Economic Belt with Central Asian Countries," September 7, 2013. As of September 20, 2021:
https://www.fmprc.gov.cn/mfa_eng/topics_665678/xjpfwzysiesgjtfhshzzfh_665686/t1076334.shtml

———, "Foreign Ministry Spokesperson Wang Wenbin's Regular Press Conference on June 10, 2021," June 10, 2021. As of September 20, 2021:
https://www.fmprc.gov.cn/mfa_eng/xwfw_665399/s2510_665401/t1882905.shtml

Nedopil, Christoph, *China's Investments in the Belt and Road Initiative in 2020: A Year of COVID-19*, Beijing, China: International Institute of Green Finance, January 2021.

North, Douglass C., "Institutions," *Journal of Economic Perspectives*, Vol. 5, No. 1, Winter 1991, pp. 97–112.

Obama, Barack, "Remarks by the President at the U.S./China Strategic and Economic Dialogue," Washington, D.C., July 27, 2009. As of November 7, 2021:
https://obamawhitehouse.archives.gov/realitycheck/the-press-office/remarks-president-uschina-strategic-and-economic-dialogue

Office of the United States Trade Representative, "The People's Republic of China: U.S.-China Trade Facts," undated. As of September 6, 2021:
https://ustr.gov/countries-regions/china-mongolia-taiwan/peoples-republic-china

Organisation for Economic Co-Operation and Development, "China's Belt and Road Initiative in the Global Trade, Investment and Finance Landscape," in *OECD Business and Finance Outlook 2018*, Paris, France: OECD Publishing, 2018.

Policy Planning Staff, Office of the Secretary of State, *The Elements of the China Challenge*, Washington, D.C., December 2020.

Posen, Barry R., "Command of the Commons: The Military Foundation of U.S. Hegemony," *International Security*, Vol. 28, No. 1, Summer 2003, pp. 5–46.

Prime, Penelope B., "China Joins the WTO: How, Why, and What Now?" *Business Economics*, Vol. 37, April 2002, pp. 26–32.

Rajah, Roland, Alexandre Dayant, and Jonathan Pryke, "Ocean of Debt? Belt and Road and Debt Diplomacy in the Pacific," Lowy Institute, October 21, 2019.

Ravelo, Jenny Lei, "DevExplains: Chinese Aid," Devex, August 17, 2017.

Rolland, Nadège, "A Concise Guide to the Belt and Road Initiative," National Bureau of Asian Research, April 11, 2019.

Rudyak, Marina, "The Ins and Outs of China's International Development Agency," Carnegie Endowment for International Peace, September 2, 2019.

Sargent, Matthew, *Mapping Cross-Border Business Networks in the Asia-Pacific Region*, Santa Monica, Calif.: RAND Corporation, RR-A792-1, 2021. As of November 18, 2021:
https://www.rand.org/pubs/research_reports/RRA792-1.html

SCO—*See* Shanghai Cooperation Organisation.

Scobell, Andrew, Edmund J. Burke, Cortez A. Cooper III, Sale Lilly, Chad J. R. Ohlandt, Eric Warner, and J. D. Williams, *China's Grand Strategy: Trends, Trajectories, and Long-Term Competition*, Santa Monica, Calif.: RAND Corporation, RR-2798-A, 2020. As of September 6, 2021:
https://www.rand.org/pubs/research_reports/RR2798.html

Shanghai Cooperation Organisation, "About SCO," webpage, undated. As of September 9, 2021:
http://eng.sectsco.org/about_sco/

Sibii, Razvan, "Grand Strategy: Government Planning," *Britannica*, undated. As of September 5, 2021:
https://www.britannica.com/topic/grand-strategy

Silberstein, Benjamin Katzeff, "The North Korean Economy, August 2019: Why China Will Continue to Dominate," *38 North*, September 10, 2019.

Silove, Nina, "Beyond the Buzzword: The Three Meanings of 'Grand Strategy,'" *Security Studies*, Vol. 27, No. 1, 2018, pp. 27–57.

Snyder, Scott A., *South Korea at the Crossroads: Autonomy and Alliance in an Era of Rival Powers*, New York: Columbia University Press, 2018.

Specialist in Asian Security Affairs, *U.S.-China Counterterrorism Cooperation: Issues for U.S. Policy*, Washington, D.C.: Congressional Research Service, RL33001, July 15, 2010.

UN—*See* United Nations.

United Nations, "Security Council–Quick Links: Veto List," webpage, October 22, 2021. As of September 20, 2021:
https://research.un.org/en/docs/sc/quick/veto

U.S. Census Bureau, "Trade in Goods with China," 2001–2021 data tables, undated. As of September 1, 2021:
https://www.census.gov/foreign-trade/balance/c5700.html

U.S. Department of Defense, *Summary of the 2018 National Defense Strategy of the United States of America: Sharpening the American Military's Competitive Edge*, Washington, D.C., 2018.

U.S. International Development Finance Corporation, *Starting Strong: A Report on DFC's First Year*, 2020 Annual Report, Washington, D.C., undated.

Vuving, Alexander L., "Grand Strategic Fit and Power Shift: Explaining Turning Points in China-Vietnam Relations," in Shiping Tang, Mingjiang Li, and Amitav Acharya, eds., *Living with China: Regional States and China Through Crises and Turning Points*, London, United Kingdom: Palgrave Macmillan, January 2009, pp. 229–245.

Walt, Vivienne, "Boxed In at the Docks: How a Lifeline from China Changed Greece," *Fortune*, July 22, 2019.

Wan, Ming, "Japan and the Asian Development Bank," *Pacific Affairs*, Vol. 68, No. 4, Winter 1995–1996, pp. 509–528.

Wang, Jisi, "China's Search for a Grand Strategy: A Rising Great Power Finds Its Way," *Foreign Affairs*, Vol. 90, No. 2, March/April 2011, pp. 68–79.

White House, "U.S.-ROK Leaders' Joint Statement," Washington, D.C., May 21, 2021.

Wit, Joel, *The United States and North Korea*, Washington, D.C.: Brookings Institution, March 15, 2001.

Xinhua News Agency, "'Belt and Road' Incorporated into CPC Constitution," October 24, 2017. As of September 20, 2021:
http://www.xinhuanet.com/english/2017-10/24/c_136702025.htm

Zheng, Sarah, "US-China Ties: Competition, Not Engagement from Now On, Kurt Campbell Says," *South China Morning Post*, May 27, 2021.

Zhou, Laura, "China Pushes for New Road and Rail Links to North Korea—and Beyond to the South," *South China Morning Post*, September 14, 2018.

Zucker, Lynne G., "Organizations as Institutions," *Research in the Sociology of Organizations*, Vol. 2, No. 1, 1983, pp. 1–47.